Integrated Studies in the Middle Grades
"Dancing Through Walls"

Integrated Studies in the Middle Grades

"Dancing Through Walls"

Edited by

Chris Stevenson and Judy F. Carr

TEACHERS COLLEGE PRESS

Teachers College, Columbia University
New York and London

Published by Teachers College Press, 1234 Amsterdam Avenue, New York, N.Y. 10027

Integrated studies in the middle grades : dancing through walls /
  edited by Chris Stevenson and Judy F. Carr.
      p.   cm.
    Includes bibliographical references and index.
    ISBN 0-8077-3220-6 (alk. paper). — ISBN 0-8077-3219-2 (pbk. :
  alk paper)
    1. Middle schools—United States—Curricula.   I. Stevenson,
  Chris.   II. Carr, Judy F.
  LB1623.5.I58   1993
  373.2'36—dc20   93-1615

#26129646

Printed on acid-free paper
Manufactured in the United States of America
99 98 97 96 95 94 93   8 7 6 5 4 3 2 1

Contents

Teachers of Uncommon Courage

For more than a century, debate has raged over whether the child or the curriculum ought to take precedence in the classrooms of our schools. John Dewey and others have tried vigorously to point out that this debate involves a false consciousness since both are necessary and, in fact, must be taken into account simultaneously if school experiences are to be truly educative. Sadly, though, these admonitions have mainly been ignored. Too many educators, to say nothing of the public, think a curriculum that appeals to the interests of young people must be frivolous or that becoming knowledgeable and skilled must be tedious. These views rest on the entirely fictitious ideas that the interests and concerns of young people are superficial, that their concerns and those of adults are at odds, that the world offers nothing of compelling interest to young people, and that knowledge and skill are only pursued for the future—that they have nothing to contribute to present life.

So it is not surprising that the focus of education throughout much of this century, particularly during the last two decades, has been marked by discussion about *how* children learn and can be made to learn, while so little attention has been paid to *what* they might learn. Now, however, conversation throughout this country (and elsewhere) is increasingly being directed toward the question: What should be the curriculum of our schools?

Most visible in the public eye is a response propelling us toward national tests and a national curriculum. Aside from the notion of nationalizing the curriculum, this is an old song. It involves prescribing sets of information drawn from various disciplines of knowledge, insisting that all young people become proficient in these areas, and administering tests to find out which ones actually do. The assumptions here are that important information and skills are invisible to the unscholarly eye, that young people have no organic interest in knowing, and that elaborate tests are necessary to "motivate" learning. Moreover, it is assumed almost blithely that knowledge and skill are "knowable" and recognizable only as they are parceled out into the separate subject compartments that academicians so conveniently construct for their specialized pursuits.

Less familiar to the public, but gaining increasing consideration, is another dimension of the current curriculum conversation. In this view, the questions and concerns of young people are seen as significant not only because they arise from real lives, but because they offer a broad-based context for the acquisition of knowledge and skill. Adults who have been able to perceive accurately the concerns of young people have been surprised to see in them echoes of their own deeply felt questions and concerns about themselves and their world. This striking similarity has led them to the conclusion that it makes no more sense to divide knowledge and skill into separate subjects in a curriculum for young people than it does to create the same divisions in learning for an adult life—where the interplay of knowledge and real life is understood to be critical.

Moreover, they understand that when the curriculum of the school engages young people in seeking answers to powerful questions about themselves and their world, and when knowledge and skill are used for this purpose, the learning that takes place is an authentic human activity requiring no tricks, gimmicks, or tests for "motivation." But more than this, they find that such activity inevitably and naturally raises possibilities for genuine valuing, cooperating, thinking, and acting.

Though this line of reasoning has been around for a long time, it has sadly fallen out of fashion in recent years. With the pressures for raising academic standards, reestablishing the priority of classical subjects, and emphasizing direct basic skills instruction, the idea of an integrated curriculum has mostly been relegated to theoretical curriculum tests, rendering it an educational direction whose potential success must largely be taken on faith alone. Now, at last, here is a book that releases the integrated curriculum from its theoretical state and brings it into real life with the documented experiences of students and teachers engaged in integrated studies. Herein are the voices of teachers as well as students describing the joys and struggles, the hopes and frustrations, and the achievements that can be derived from what remains for many merely a topic of conjecture. For this reason alone, this book has an authority that cannot be ignored.

Beyond this, however, these stories take place in a particular context, namely the middle grades. This does not mean that there is no message for those interested in elementary and high schools—indeed, there is. But this is the level of schooling that has come under so much scrutiny lately because it involves young people who are in that dramatic and ambiguous period of life called early adolescence, when so much of life seems to hang precariously in the balance. This is a time when questions and concerns about identity, values, justice, belonging, and so on are particularly heightened. Likewise, it is a time when a curriculum that is removed from such concerns seems especially abstract and irrelevant.

This is not to say that middle level educators have been altogether insensitive to these issues. Over the past thirty years of the middle school movement, and even before that in some parts of the junior high school movement, efforts have been made to move beyond the separate subject curriculum toward making connections among the various subjects, becoming more sensitive to who these young people are, and bending the traditions of the institution to make it more inviting to youth. Yet even as these success stories are told, many middle level educators recognize that their work has not gone as far as it should nor has it resolved the continuing tension between teachers and young people.

So it is that many middle level educators have begun to ask questions about the curriculum of their schools. At the heart of the discussion is the realization that the creation of a genuine middle school curriculum ought to begin with the young people who represent, according to the rhetoric of the middle school movement, the primary concern of these schools. And these educators are beginning to discover again the idea of integration in the curriculum; that is, not just subject areas, but the possibility of helping early adolescents formulate and seek answers to their questions, reflect on possible answers, and integrate these experiences into their scheme of meanings.

This is not an easy thing to do. In fact, for many teachers it is a painful experience, involving as it does the letting go of so much of what they have done for so long. Worse yet, they soon realize that there is no conveniently packaged curriculum, no recipe, no set of handouts. Aside from a nearly lost history of similar work, there is little but their own imagination, courage, and respect for young people to guide them. Now we have this book, *Integrated Studies in the Middle Grades: "Dancing Through Walls."* Still there is no recipe—in doing this kind of curriculum there never can be. But there are stories here from other teachers that tell us it is possible, that it can be done. When we read them we know that we are not alone. Others share our vision and the struggle that goes along with it. If they can do it, perhaps we can too. In this sense, the "dance" in this book gives us what we need.

At present, the idea of national tests and a national curriculum is proving to be a seductive one. It is simplistic and easily propagandized through clever slogan systems. Its support by politicians and business executives has the power to frighten parents and others in local communities about their own childrens' fate if they do not "volunteer" to participate in the national project. But that power only obscures the weak educational reasoning behind this unresponsive and irresponsible approach to education. On the other hand, the concept of an integrated curriculum is a relatively complicated one. It sounds too unlike the curriculum that most adults experienced in their own school days. It requires the messy necessity of listening to young people and thinking about how and what they learn. It defies simple quantitative assessments and letter-grade report cards. In other words, it breaks away from the traditions so many adults have come to know, and which are far easier to keep than to change, no matter how undesirable they may be.

Thus the work of those who advocate an integrated curriculum is not only educational. It is political as well. To resist the powerful push for a prescribed, separate subject curriculum and related tests is no easy thing to do. To risk the wrath of unsympathetic school officials and apprehensive parents is both personally and professionally dangerous. By understanding this we can see clearly that the experiences documented in this book, and others like them, are not only records of wonderful, successful educational events—they are larger than that. These are the stories of teachers of uncommon courage.

What is it that leads these teachers to care so deeply about young people that they are willing to set aside the usual arrangements of school to do something so special? How is it that they can hear so well the voices of the young? What led them to believe that the projects they describe here would be as marvelous as they turned out to be? What attracted them to accept the invitation to participate in this project? Where did they get the attitudes, the knowledge, and the skill to do what they did? If only we knew the answers to these questions, perhaps we could do better in helping new teachers prepare to be with young people. How much better our schools would be.

For the moment, though, perhaps we should just savor the stories in this book, recognize the options they create for our schools, and let them inspire us. For these contributions alone, surely we should be thankful for the teachers who have told their stories.

James A. Beane
Professor
National College of Education
National-Louis University

Acknowledgments

The teacher-authors whose work is found in this book have emulated the vision, determination, and hard work that are "professionalism." They worked earnestly through the heat and humidity of summer days which they'd surely have delighted in spending at the beach. They gave up Saturdays during the fall semester to share and critique their work. They persisted on their manuscripts through multiple edits, striving to tell their stories just right. We have benefited from their insights about their young adolescent students, and we have been inspired regularly by their ongoing commitment to meaningful education for their kids. We could not have had better colleagues in this project, and we are forever grateful to them and for them.

Ken Bergstrom has been particularly close to this collaboration. His wisdom about children and their learning is especially evident in his description of the Winooski River study (chapter 10). He made substantial contributions beyond that chapter, however, by sharing his enlightenment and reflections about teaching. Much of the material in chapter 2 and the Epilogue derive from Ken's perceptions. We deeply appreciate his readiness to listen, reflect, and share, and we cherish a friendship that has prospered through this work.

Jim Beane and Gordon Vars freely gave us ample portions of inspiration and assurance. Nancy Berliner's thoughtful comments helped us immeasurably during the final editing stages. Donna Rowe of the University of Vermont could not have been more responsive to our needs for technical expertise. And no one could have been more dependable, prompt, and cheerful than Donna in expediting multiple rewrites of various sections of the manuscript.

Finally, we wish to thank Katherine Stevenson and Tom Carr for their patience, confidence, and support as we brought this adventure to completion.

Introduction

An Invitation to Dance

Chris Stevenson and Judy F. Carr

In this, my thirteenth year of teaching, I believe I will devote more time to integrated studies. I've become convinced that less is actually more. An in-depth study allows for more and richer learning than does a cursory overview of an entire single subject. I am ready to repress that "ghost of subject coverage" that haunted me for years. It is unreasonable to expect early adolescents to conceptualize the span of an entire discipline when they have yet to explore the depths of their own learning potential. I will continue to influence the school curriculum to reflect concepts and skills that facilitate interdisciplinary study rather than impede it by focusing on content and subject requirements.

The essence of teaching lies beyond surviving in the classroom, beyond classroom management concerns, beyond curriculum content and process, and even beyond the developmental needs of students. The best middle grades teaching results from simply understanding individual students with the mind and the heart—it is an act of love.

So, despite the restrictions of my teaching environment, despite the suspicions of others that I'm not "covering" enough material, I will continue to use interdisciplinary study to create a meaningful, healthy and loving learning atmosphere for my students. I want them to wonder, dream, invent, struggle, argue, inquire, design, imagine, fail, rethink, succeed, and learn to love life and learning. Interdisciplinary study is the best approach to help me—and them—to reach these ends.

Ken Bergstrom[1]

The subtitle of this book, *"Dancing Through Walls,"* is deliberate. If learners and teachers in the middle grades are to realize their fullest potential, we most remove lots of "walls"—the mental barriers that derive from a textbook–workbook–recitation–test orientation to instruction; the submission to vague pressures to "cover" one curriculum or another; the isolation of colleagues in different disciplines; incongruities between child-development theory and prevalent instructional practices. These ineffective yet seemingly intractable rituals not only waste precious opportunities and kids' time, but they also thwart or kill outright teachers' imagination and courage to innovate.

Youngsters in the middle grades are going through personal changes that dramatically affect their dispositions toward school learning. They enthusiastically embrace opportunities for firsthand exploration of the world beyond the classroom where astute teachers can help them make all kinds of connections between experiential learning and more conventional scholarship. They hunger to learn *how* to learn in ways that transcend traditional classroom routines confined to textbooks, workbooks, ditto sheets, and recitations about discipline-specific content usually unrelated to their interests and questions. And, especially, kids need teachers who embody optimism and imagination as they create innovative curriculum calculated to correspond more closely to the needs of their young adolescent constituents.

Over the last two decades, public and professional attention has increasingly been turned toward the education of young adolescents. That interest has evolved into what is frequently touted as the "middle school movement." An emerging research agenda is being identified and explored, and professional literature about the education of young adolescents has grown steadily for more than two decades. National, regional, and state organizations have been formed to disseminate exemplary practices. More than half of the states have added middle level teacher certification and created support services for these teachers. In spite of all of this encouraging activity, however, the question of middle grades curriculum has not been widely addressed by practitioners.

Throughout the literature concerned with the education of young adolescents (ages 10–14) are references to the propriety of curricular studies that (1) combine disciplines, (2) focus on topics of natural interest to youngsters, and (3) explicitly address their transitional nature as learners. There are few documented examples of successfully implemented studies that address any one of these criteria, and studies that integrate all three criteria are virtually nonexistent. Yet, every middle grades teacher continues to face the essential dilemma of how to create schooling that truly educates kids—that informs them; that makes sense to them; that increases their personal power as learners; that more closely matches their individual proclivities and dispositions as learners. We believe this challenge is and will always remain intensely personal—the essence of teaching.

It is now time to move beyond surface features to substantive curricular change in middle level education. Many middle level schools across the country are well on the way to full implementation of interdisciplinary team organization, teacher advisory programs, and block scheduling. But all too often that block schedule is subsequently redivided into 35- to 42-minute classes, and team planning time is likewise often used to discuss logistical details or "problem students" rather than collaborative curriculum design. In fact, most middle level teachers continue to describe themselves as a "science teacher" or an "English teacher"; their academic programs continue to be conceived mainly as "courses" that "cover" content and skills that are prescribed by external guides or textbooks and which, presumably, are needed for success in high school. That this is the case speaks to the power of tradition, the uncertainty of the unknown, and our failure, individually and collectively, to proffer substantive alternatives and challenges to the status quo.

Now is also the time for middle level educators to give ourselves permission to truly *explore* the transitional intellectual and psychosocial character of young adolescent students in order that we might create responsive curriculum for them. Doing so will lead us into "writing new tunes and dancing new steps." Yes, it's scary business sometimes, but, more importantly, it is *necessary* work that will be accomplished more expeditiously and successfully by working together rather than alone.

Three years ago we invited some three dozen middle grades teachers to consider joining us in designing, teaching, and writing about curriculum created to be responsive to our students' developmental nature and needs. Using easily accessible topics for study, we proposed that together we design some studies based upon what we knew about how kids develop and learn during their middle years. Two thirds of the group joined us, and this book tells about that work—the new tunes and steps that were its product .

These teachers were well experienced with traditional ways of schooling in the middle grades, and many had already taken initiatives in their respective schools to create "alternative" multiage programs with names such as Alpha, Odyssey, Protostar, and the like. But they also wanted much more. They wanted to do studies that would be likely to win genuine commitments from their kids, studies that would offer so many options that every single student could "work at his or her own level." In brief, they were ready for serious curriculum innovation—to explore some compelling possibilities that would extend them and their students.

This book recounts the personal journeys of these personally and professionally committed Vermont middle grades teachers in several different school settings—K–6, 6–8, and 7–12—as they worked their way through this essential challenge. Together we studied the literature describing the variety of changes our 10- to 14-year-olds were undergoing. Then we invented strategies calculated to create matches between those descriptions and our perceptions of our particular students. At the same time we assessed our communities for topics for potential study that would also be likely to interest our kids. Finally, we undertook the most critical challenge of all—designing teaching plans that integrated all these elements. This adventure took us into some pedagogical territory that most of us had not previously explored.

From the beginning, our purpose was to "experiment" by responsibly pursuing what seemed to us to be sound ideas about how and what young adolescents might learn. Throughout the project there were especially memorable occasions when teachers showed that wonderful excitement of realizing they were on to something. At follow-up sharing sessions on Saturdays, they took turns sharing their projects in an atmosphere where the pride and reciprocal professional respect were palpable.

We believe that this is a book for all teachers who work with young adolescents. It affirms and, we hope, will extend, the efforts of those who are already daring to dance. We also expect that this book will help awaken and hearten other teachers to challenge their assumed barriers—to join the dance. We invite all readers who know the exigencies of educating children in transition and who wish for more than the ordinary, to consider our experience, and then to create their own.

NOTES

[1]Excerpted from Ken Bergstrom's unpublished journal.

1

PICKING THE TUNES AND CHOOSING THE STEPS

Chapter 1

Goals for Integrated Studies

Chris Stevenson and Judy F. Carr

> We have asked what it means to become adolescent. Were school peo-
> ple to become engaged in this question, the implications for schooling
> would be radical.
>
> Lipsitz, 1977, p. 84

Throughout the literature about the education of 10- to 14-year-old
students are references to the propriety of curricular studies that
address explicitly the transitional nature and needs of young adolescent learners, focus on topics of natural interest to them, and combine
traditional disciplines (NMSA, 1982; NASSP, 1985; Carnegie, 1989).
These students are intensely curious about their world and themselves,
and by virtue of biological and cultural influences during these years,
these students are continually changing and evolving as learners. Common sense argues that virtually all day-to-day experiences in these
youngsters' lives are inherently interdisciplinary.

Although appeals for exploratory curricula and interdisciplinary
teaching are welcome, they have not been backed up by nearly enough
direction, definition, or examples. A large part of the explanation of
this failure to reconceptualize middle grade curriculum and instruction around youngsters' developmental traits lies in the difficulty in
defining early adolescence in terms that dictate specific pedagogy. A

single child's development at any moment in time represents a complex of physical, cognitive, and psychosocial changes that occur on an idiosyncratic schedule. And although all youngsters change quite a lot over the early adolescent years, there is also extensive variability among them.

Just as young adolescents are developmentally different, they also come from diverse backgrounds. The pluralistic composition of contemporary American society is clearly reflected in the children who populate our schools. Race and ethnicity may be most evident at first glance, but more subtle yet equally definitive individual differences exist, such as family composition and structure, parenting styles, religion, and economic circumstances. And where cultural diversity is seen as a cornerstone of our melting-pot society, that same diversity can also be divisive. Left unattended by sensitive, responsive adults, kids may draw lines of inclusion and exclusion according to such diversity.

In this period of developmental differences and cultural diversity, young adolescents have an urgent need to define themselves as individuals and to belong to something they acknowledge as good. Even in rural and small-town Vermont, we have come to appreciate the significance of our students' diverse backgrounds. A third of our population has roots in Quebec, and there is a distinct Abenaki Indian heritage across the state. Many of our communities were settled by immigrants from Ireland, Scotland, Italy, and Spain and reflect those ethnic roots. Vermont's composition has become further diversified in more recent decades due to immigration from Asian countries, notably Vietnam and Korea, and an influx of city dwellers who are seeking the more bucolic life associated with rural New England. Even though the state's population is overwhelmingly Caucasian, ethnic and family traditions are often quite distinctive, and differences in socioeconomic circumstances are substantial.

We felt a pressing need to create a curriculum that would draw all our students together around purposes and tasks that could be shared, transcending the background differences that can so easily become divisive and destructive to the kind of learning climate in which students can make meaningful personal investments. We believe that every youngster embodies a potential for unique, even idiosyncratic, contributions to the work of the group. We thought that by integrating traditional subject matter with students' individual interests, we could enhance the quality of interpersonal life for a class or team.

One can correctly argue that developmental changes and sociocultural differences are not unique to early adolescence and have parallels throughout life. An essential distinction during early adolescence is, however, that consciousness about personal change is unprecedented in these youngsters' lives. They are inexperienced and lack familiarity with many of the feelings, ideas, and decisions they now confront. These are tender years in which most youngsters are facing many of the realities and complexities of the actual world for the first time. That is not to say that they have not been exposed to these complexities. The difference now is that in the midst of their own extensive transitions, they are increasingly aware of the complexities and, therefore, uniquely vulnerable in their initial efforts to understand and cope with them.

As many of them become more aware, they also become more receptive to experimentation with new opportunities. For example, regardless of what an adult's attitude may be toward an adolescent's first love, the youngster's thoughts are easily and naturally dominated by thoughts of the beloved. Grown-ups may dismiss this as puppy love, but it is nonetheless very intense and often has a profound effect on the day-to-day life of the novice. The young adolescent's vulnerability to the dangers of experimentation with tobacco, alcohol, and other addictive drugs is likewise increased by new curiosities bolstered by the naiveté that "I can handle it; it won't hurt me." We believed that we needed to acknowledge the magnitude and intensity of our students' change process, all the while seeking ways to respond to and complement emerging new needs and inquisitiveness in healthy, age-appropriate ways.

We were additionally concerned that young adolescents today are growing up in a world that simultaneously expects far more and far less of them than in the past. We are aware that one and two centuries ago most 12-year-olds had a specific purpose in their lives: They worked a full share as laborers on the family farm, they worked in mines and factories, or they apprenticed to craftsmen. No reasonable person would wish to see today's young adolescents returned full-time to such roles. On the other hand, however, perhaps our society has overreacted to traditional forms of child exploitation by removing children from opportunities to learn that are available only through first-hand engagement of the actual world. Perhaps we have mistakenly insulated children too much from that context, failing to salvage valuable opportunities for learning that are unavailable in traditional classroom-bound schooling. In our eagerness to protect children from misuse, have we created a no-person's-land for our youngsters caught between childhood and young adulthood—our "in-betweeners"?

Changes in family composition and parents' employment add further to uncertainty about children's place. Many if not most kids are dependent on parents or other adults to transport them, give them money, and schedule their lives while parents are working. Kids appear to be spending much of this opportune time suspended between childhood and adulthood, waiting to engage the real world around them but having very little real authority over what they do and how they spend their time. They lack much opportunity for taking on real responsibility in the world of work, and there are few established ways they can provide useful service to the adult world. Like substitute players on an athletic team, these youngsters wait interminably for an opportunity to join the game, even briefly. Sadly, too many lack meaningful work experience before they enter adulthood.

Now more than ever, our nation seems to need people who are capable of and disposed toward taking responsibility for themselves, each other, and our planet. We need problem solvers who are optimists, lifelong learners who grow continuously in their understanding and initiatives toward the common good, whole humans who are good citizens. For such a long time, school has been thought of rather obliquely as preparation for adult life, with the implication being that simply surviving school is enough. We believe that school can be more than that. Rather than reflect society as it is, we want schooling to introduce our students to learning as it is when it is best: intriguing, challenging, and fulfilling. We believe that the best preparation for adult life is life lived well in childhood, especially the crucial years of early adolescence.

Finally, we were influenced by our awareness that we are preparing our students for a world very different from that which we have known. Some absolute certainties about these youngsters' futures that we acknowledge are:

- They will need to know how to find and use the resources they need.
- They will need to function in a technological society.
- They will need to assert their responsibility for themselves, their communities, and their world.

WHY INTEGRATED STUDIES?

Traditionally, the middle-level curriculum has been organized around subject matter designations. Mathematics, language arts, science, and social studies have been regarded as core subjects. Students also commonly have classes in subjects often referred to as exploratories; foreign languages, studio arts, music, home economics, and industrial arts fall under that designation. The school day is customarily organized into eight to ten periods of anywhere from 30 minutes to an hour's length in order to accommodate these different subjects. This familiar organizational structure descended to the middle level from high school and college, and we were quite aware that it was not in any way grounded in what is known about the cognitive and personal development of young adolescents. From the beginning, we recognized the learning and teaching limitations of following deductive, prescriptive curricula organized around teaching priorities that didn't appear to consider at all the developmental nature of the learners.

The most notable literature concerned with student-centered learning at this level argues for interdisciplinary curriculum (NMSA, 1982; NASSP, 1985; Carnegie, 1989; Beane, 1990). In such studies, distinctions between specific disciplines are supposed to blur, often disappearing altogether. At their best, such units blend students' ideas and interests about the topic with general and discipline-specific resources. Many schools in Vermont and beyond have explored a variety of curricular studies that have been called interdisciplinary. Most of what we have seen has actually been multidisciplinary, however. A typical scenario has teachers of various subject areas agreeing on a topic or theme and then separately implementing discipline-specific strategies in their separate classes. Reading *Johnny Tremaine* in language arts class while studying the Revolutionary War in social studies is an example of what we have seen being done under the rubric of interdisciplinary curriculum. Teachers often had to struggle to fit math or science into a unit in equal balance with the other subjects, which inevitably resulted in contrivances that were self-evidently *not* interdisciplinary but multidisciplinary. We saw this outcome as tantamount to teachers "working alone together" without much regard for whether the unit was responsive to students' ideas and questions.

On the other hand, what we elected to call integrated studies began with our students and a selected topic or theme that was obviously or likely to be interesting to them. The resulting rightness of fit between that topic choice and subsequently planned learning activities derived directly from the students' contexts. Once that design was conceptualized, aspects of many disciplines were identified and included. It was not an either-or proposition but a matter of priorities. Kids' ideas, interests, and questions came first; prescribed content and skills were secondary. For example, two teachers who had previously specialized in language arts and science planned a study of death in our culture because of some occurrences in their town and their students' resulting concerns and questions (see chapter 15). As neither teacher was an expert on the matter, they piggybacked on each other's observations and ideas. They quickly discovered a need for resources outside their subject specializations, and as a consequence of their commitment to the study, potential turf concerns never materialized.

We reasoned that if the work our youngsters undertook was to be truly authentic, it had to be relevant. The education that derived from the units we planned should reflect balance between their contexts and what we as teachers know they need to know and be able to do. This key notion about integration promised that our students would become personally engaged in their learning.

OUR GOALS

Our overall goals for integrated study in the middle grades were based not only on an understanding of expectations associated with various subject matters but also on our understanding of the kids themselves, their observations about the world they inhabit, and our expectations of qualities and competencies that today's youth needs now and for the future. Although our goals may not be particularly new or different, the importance of making them explicit among ourselves cannot be overstated. Inherent in these goals are what we recognize as clear implications for innovation in the form of an integrated approach toward curriculum.

Goal 1: Students Will Grow More Confident

Feeling positive and confident about oneself can be hard to accomplish when change is so constant among one's peers and there is uncertainty about what personal changes will come next. Perhaps the most familiar example of such variability in early adolescence is seen in widely ranging differences in youngsters' physical development. Although physical growth spurts generally occur earlier for girls than for boys, individuals do not experience growth acceleration at the same time as their same-age peers. Similarly, they do not grow through their physical changes at the same pace. Youngsters of the same chronological age may have vastly differing physical makeup—creating the false impression that they are several years apart in age.

An intensified preoccupation with how one appears to oneself and subsequently to others has much to do with self-perception. Those of us who spend lots of time with these children recognize and respect this time of intensified self-examination. Often we are called on to reassure a child who thinks her nose is too big or fears her complexion will never clear up. The ambivalences that children feel about their more adultlike bodies—on the one hand welcoming these changes and on the other being apprehensive about what will happen next—can be a continuing challenge to self-confidence.

Corresponding differences in psychological development may be less visible, but they are nonetheless distinct and influential in their effects on youngsters' lives. Ten- and 11-year-olds are inclined to describe themselves in terms of what they can do. Being a worker, being a producer, and being known by others by and for those traits become increasingly important to healthy identity development. Youngsters need to see that they are improving in skills and accomplishments sanctioned as part of being a good student. Children also prize the concrete evidence of their accomplishments—whether it is a 100% correct spelling test or a bookshelf constructed in woodworking class. Successful participation in a concert, a sports activity, or a play or a successful presentation to other students or parents provides tangible evidence that not only is the work meritorious but also that "I am a worthwhile person."

The child's need for recognition and approval from classmates is especially strong; it may become even stronger than corresponding desires for approval from parents or teachers. During these years, children are also especially vulnerable to peer disapproval, and self-confidence may be shattered by peer rejection.

Nevertheless, expectations, opportunities, and standards in the instructional program must be broad and varied enough that they are within the grasp of all children in the class. As variability is so wide and so crucial a concern at this time, there must be options and choices that will accommodate even the widest ranges of children's differences and idiosyncrasies—including mainstreamed students. Failure to achieve healthy identity development produces alienation, withdrawal, and antagonism, which are all too familiar.

Lack of recognition when one is attempting to do the right thing and be successful provokes feelings of inferiority. When a school's recognition system is limited to competitive awards such as an honor roll and individual athletic awards, only a few children receive the recognition all of them need. Competition is, after all, restrictive. Children who do not receive these kinds of awards or equivalent recognition from classmates and adults are unnecessarily subject to enormous risk of believing "I can't do," and, therefore, "I am not as worthwhile as the others." This familiar pattern often raises an emotionally charged but false controversy for many people: that the way to provide recognition for all students is to lower standards. The key ingredient in this discussion is that children know they are improving in ways endorsed by teachers and other adults. Compliments that come from others who help celebrate accomplishments are the ribbon on the gift. How unfortunate but commonplace it is to encounter children only 10 and 11 years old who speak of their inadequacy and mediocrity, demean their own schoolwork, and have already accepted that they aren't good students—that is, good learners!

The urgency of children's self-confidence and personal efficacy can hardly be overstated. They have a formidable task in learning about themselves and how their world functions at a time when they and their friends are also experiencing so much change. They hunger for opportunities to show what they can do and also for recognition for their accomplishments. And this is not merely a transient need that may be sated by a single success. During these critical years, children need continuous successes and recurring recognition. They are living through a period of continuing vulnerability to failure and self-doubt. Our task as teachers is to devise ways in which they can satisfy these hungers, helping them to become convinced that they are capable and praiseworthy. Who knows how often children who regularly encounter failure and who receive little or no approval from peers, parents, and teachers develop a deep-seated belief that they are incapable of learning and performing successfully—and, in time, fulfill this personal theory? Our task as teachers is gigantic, for we must help each student know what it means to be successful, worthwhile in the sight of others, and optimistic about personal prospects.

Anxieties surrounding identity definition intensify in the early adolescent years, and that intensity may persist for only a few years or, regrettably, for as long as a lifetime. For the identity formation process to be complete, the individual successfully reworks previous needs of trust, autonomy, and initiative (Erikson, 1968). Through this process, a revised sense of self emerges that enables one to function comfortably and effectively in multiple roles.

Emerging adolescents also begin to think in more formal intellectual terms about many of the social, personal, and ethical issues in their surroundings. A new awareness of the ideal comes into play, and it is common for adolescents to compare their own circumstances with an idealized vision of how life might be. A common indication of this awareness is evidence that a young person is thinking theoretically, that is, making theories to explain or justify how things are or how they might be. There is also a tendency toward forming cliques in which an individual may define oneself in terms of the attributes of the chosen group. Those attributes may be fashion or dress, language, heroes, ideals, habits, or life-style.

Healthy identity definition derives from an integration of everything youngsters have learned about themselves from the assortment of roles they have filled: child, grandchild, sibling, pal, student, athlete, and so on. The answer to "Who am I?" emerges from an idiosyncratic consolidation of past and current role definitions. Role confusion may persist well on into adulthood when identity definition during middle and late adolescence has not been successfully resolved. Quite obviously, the urgency of a child's need to perceive himself or herself in a positive light has direct implications on how educational experiences are conceived and organized. Too many students pass through these years never seeing themselves as positive, contributing members of their school community. An affirmative, optimistic view of oneself as a learner and as a person must become the foremost goal of schooling— especially in the middle grades. Our integrated studies focused on this urgent, paramount goal by providing a wide variety of ways in which students could contribute to a shared study according to their individual interests and talents.

Goal 2: Students Will Work Together Cooperatively

Teachers have long recognized the power of relationships that draw students into close cooperation and commitment to a shared project. In athletics, it is particularly easy to see that a team is successful because the members play well together. We hoped to create integrated curriculum designs that would promote synergism among our students as well as between them and the adults whom their studies would enlist. We expected that working with adults other than the classroom teacher would further enhance our students' belief in the importance of their work.

The evolution of close peer relationships during the few years of early adolescence is marked by a gradually increasing intensity. Easy-come, easy-go friendships typical of 10-year-olds often begin to be replaced by the more exacting alliances we're more accustomed to seeing when they're several years older. Friendship agendas change in both quality and intensity. Worry about peer relationships increases and intensifies over the middle grades. One study reported that although school performance and physical appearance were the most frequently cited sources of worry among young adolescents, worry about relationships with friends is also high. Furthermore, these three sources of worry are the only ones that increase as children pass through the middle grades. Quite obviously, youngsters need lots of opportunities to learn how to relate to each other and how to work together cooperatively in these years of change if they are to manage successfully friendships and other social needs, both now and later in life.

The middle grade years also witness significant change in relationships between girls and boys. Children just beginning to accelerate their movement into this stage around ages 10 and 11 are, for the most part, primarily interested in same-sex friendships and peer groups. Sometimes boy-girl friendships exist, but more typically boys elect to spend their time with boys, and girls stay with girls. As they move further through this developmental phase, however, they increasingly acknowledge and attend to each other. Often there is an awkward self-consciousness about reaching out to the opposite sex, and the label "sweethearts" usually provokes embarrassment, sometimes followed by vigorous denial. How significant become the changes they experience by 13 and 14! Regardless of how much any individual actually pursues a romantic liaison in these grades, the girl-boy issue is clearly on the table.

We appreciate the emotional power of girl-boy relationships in this transitional time, and we must be committed to establishing and preserving a school atmosphere that protects children from pressures to grow up faster than necessary in terms of social and romantic sophistication. Perhaps the soundest policy is one that seeks a moratorium on kids "going with" each other, dating, going to dances, and so on. Although it is not our business to suppress romantic alliances, we need to identify ways in which boys and girls can spend time together comfortably while developing friendships free from premature pressures and expectations. A certain way to accomplish this is to form a variety of groupings irrespective of gender in which the emphasis is on collaboration to accomplish shared purposes.

Although we cannot tidily dissect and analyze the identity formation process, we do recognize that children benefit only from favorable status among both their peer groups and among their older adolescent and adult contacts. Simply being assigned to being a member of a peer group guarantees nothing more than certainty of momentary social belonging—assuming the student is willing to participate in a particular group in the first place. The key element in grouping is that every student functions in a variety of capacities or roles over an extended period of time—say, several weeks. It is very desirable for every student to experience leading and learning how to lead as well as being a good follower. It is valuable for every child to know that he or she can lead others.

It is basic to acknowledge the weight of the influence of peer groups during these years. Peers often take over the authority formerly enjoyed by parents or teachers as the primary influence in a youngster's life. Children with substantial identity confusion are likely to take on the characteristics of groups in which they seek membership. With groups that are alienated from schooling, group identification is usually destructive to independent identity formation. Such groups are familiar to us in virtually all schools because they are usually known by stereotyped labels such as nerds, preppies, jocks, brains, druggies, dummies, do-gooders, and so on. Children who are particularly needy in psychosocial terms and who become members of these groups may subjugate personal standards to group norms and expectations. For example, if one group is characterized by doing schoolwork well, individuals within the group will perform accordingly. Conversely, the ethic for a macho group is that members should have machismo.

An issue of enormous urgency in early adolescent education is, thus, the development of both the disposition and skills necessary for positive, successful interpersonal relationships as well as a healthy individual identity. This constituted our second fundamental goal for integrated studies.

Goal 3: Students Will Develop Social-Ethical Consciousness

Today's children are protected from the child labor exploitation of the past. No thinking person would challenge the importance of that protection. However, in removing children from the workplace, we have also isolated our students from an important source of learning: supportive adults outside the classroom who emulate exemplary citizenship. In protecting children from the abuses of the past, we have also unwittingly eliminated or reduced their opportunities to learn from side-by-side interactions with adults from the farm, the factory, the professions, and the marketplace.

We recognize that many of our students' coaches, relatives, and neighbors and other adult community members besides ourselves can be instrumental in helping our students to learn well. As teachers, we are in a position to use our students' eagerness to work together as a basis for creating many different small-group configurations. Those small groups then bring our kids the chance to work with other adults in an assortment of combinations. For these projects, we sought to cultivate constructive relationships with trustworthy adults in our communities.

Young adolescents today lack adequate role definition that corresponds to their needs for personal empowerment and responsibility.

David Elkind laments the dissolution of markers—"external signs of where we stand" (1984, p. 93). Just a couple of decades ago, children wore children's clothes that were distinct from the styles preferred by adolescents. Today, fashion for students of all ages is far less distinct. Organized, uniformed athletic teams were formerly reserved for high school, yet today, children in primary schools may be part of an organized team that practices and plays regularly scheduled games with other similarly organized teams. There are even beauty contests for children from the toddler age right up through the preteens and beyond. Traditionally, markers confirmed for the child and everyone else the progress he or she had achieved to date in the extended process of growing to full adult maturity. The activity, clothing, authority, and image markers of past generations that Elkind describes made it much more possible to identify just how much independence a youngster had earned. In our contemporary culture, however, such distinctions have become blurred, and neither youngsters nor adults seem to be very clear about or agree on their understanding of just what is wise and appropriate to expect of young adolescents.

Another consequence of this separation is that young adolescents have few opportunities to perform service of real benefit to others. Meanwhile, adolescents urgently "need to be needed," as Charity James expresses it (1974, p. 44). Today's youngsters also live in a world in which the resolution of such problems as pollution, world hunger, and threats of war beg for dialogue, with active participation by everyone. Yet time apportioned for service to others is scarce. Kids waste vast amounts of time watching television or just "hanging out." Even the most privileged children are preoccupied with private lessons of all kinds and team sports activities. Although these may certainly be valuable activities, they leave little time for kids to do things that are worthwhile and beneficial to others. To paraphrase the title of an important book about adolescent psychosocial development, kids are "all grown up with nothing particularly worthwhile to do" (Elkind, 1984). Meanwhile, 10- to 14-year-olds have grown and developed enough to take on meaningful responsibility for their families, neighborhoods, schools, and communities.

People judge and choose throughout their lives. Young children appear to be driven by immediacy: They look quickly and choose quickly. But as they begin to mature intellectually, they are increasingly able to examine choices more analytically and objectively than had been possible before. They are able to reason through "what is best for me" and "what is best for everyone." Consequences become more clearly foreseeable. These middle grades of school are, therefore, an opportune time for us to lead students into choosing and decision making that are based more than ever before on the merits and demerits inherent in the options they face. It is during these few years, in fact, that many children make major decisions that often have far-reaching consequences, especially in life-style experimentations.

One of the most intriguing characteristics of children in these years is their propensity for what are essentially existential questions: Who am I? What am I supposed to do? We can sometimes observe them "thinking out loud" about profound questions. Occasionally, we witness them appearing to figure out what they believe—at least for the moment—by hearing themselves talk about an issue. Children's theories reflect their perceptions and ideas about what is meaningful in their lives. Such speculations can be useful in understanding the development of thinking as well as of personal identity. Alternative explanations, multiple solutions to a problem, assertions that are contrary to fact—all these fully human deliberations become increasingly accessible to young adolescents pondering their existence. From all of this thought, personal principles may emerge even if they are articulated only to settle a momentary issue.

It was, therefore, especially important in these integrated studies for us to help our students come to grips with some of their beliefs, inclinations, and questions in a context that both honors individual expression and appreciates that such ideas will evolve over the course of time and human experience. We sought opportunities for students to come to grips with selected aspects of contemporary life that are both within their conceptual grasp and directly related to their developing belief systems.

"I was wrong. I blew it that time. I lost my concentration." These statements acknowledge the speaker's error or failure. Looking at or into oneself and accepting what is there without self-condemnation is mature introspection. The youngster who honestly acknowledges that "I used to hate you, but now I like you" is dealing responsibly with a personal change that is familiar to most of us: forgiving oneself. It is also important for kids to figure out their role and status vis-à-vis family, peer groups, and adults. Intense feelings—especially about these interpersonal matters—are common to kids. Learning to acknowledge and deal with one's intense feelings as factors in living and learning can be enhanced when youngsters are encouraged to accept themselves as they are for the moment while working deliberately on issues that continue to be disquieting.

Much has been written about children's moral development. They certainly have lots of beliefs about what is right and wrong. Sometimes moral imperatives come from religion, especially when children express beliefs in terms of particular sectarian positions. Young adolescents are increasingly capable of recognizing and appreciating higher truths. This is also a time of life characterized by kids' conceptualization of the ideal, the perfect world. Positions on right or wrong often derive from their judgment of an ideal that transcends actuality. Many of their beliefs derive from events that they or others close to them experience firsthand—especially ones that leave significant marks, even emotional scars.

Discrimination in social relationships is a particularly sensitive matter to young adolescents, who are especially vulnerable to rejection from another person they admire. The rejection may generate energy around very idealistic beliefs, especially in their thoughts about loyalty and betrayal. There are also occasions when children are able to be philosophical about their experience: "Well, that's the way the cookie crumbles." This ability to transcend conventional reactions—to keep going with renewed energy when events haven't worked out to personal expectations or satisfaction—enables a youngster to become more self-sufficient than remaining fixed in self-pity. Children can be remarkably helpful to each other in such circumstances, and integrated studies provide enhanced opportunities for them to provide mutual support as they engage in socially responsible decision making and take action.

Goal 4: Students Will Think, Think, and Think

Exercise in thinking increases intellectual strength, competence, and resilience as surely as calisthenics develop the body. Games, puzzles, and simulations are not only enjoyable, but as kids experience success, they learn to transfer game skills to more reality-based situations. Lots of experience that requires systematic thinking help youngsters to grow and develop into increasingly efficient thinkers: self-sufficient problem solvers, skilled organizers, and discriminating critics. Practice expands and improves these abilities.

They need learning situations that include lots of opportunities for them to manifest their ideas and speculations. Their tangible work constitutes trustworthy indicators of how well they are progressing through developmental intellectual tasks. And in using the term *indicators*, we are not referring to standardized tests or kits that purport to develop and evaluate so-called thinking skills. Although such measures may reveal useful data about more passive thought, it is through what children actually conceive, organize, do, and present to us and others that their intellectual functioning can be seen and understood most clearly.

Attentive observation and thought occur together. Therefore, learning how to observe thoroughly and see holistically as well are essential functions of the mind from infancy. One dimension of the intellectual changes that young adolescents are experiencing is their growing capacity to represent their observations through outward manifestations of thought: speaking, writing, drawing, planning, organizing, constructing, and presenting. These processes reveal both general intellectual development as well as individual talents and proclivities.

One of the most direct reflections of a student's thought is simply what he or she says. Of course, available time in the school day doesn't provide an opportunity for daily one-on-one interviews with very many students. However, regularly scheduled presentations are an excellent way for students to learn how to organize and present what they think and know, providing their teachers with regular exposure to this particular window into their understanding. One teacher who commuted 40 minutes to school each day established a classroom schedule for students to tape-record a 5- to 10-minute report on their work. The teacher then listened to the tapes on her commute and, in turn, tape-recorded her responses to each student's comments while occasionally adding specific suggestions.

Another important and primary reflection of children's thought is, of course, their writing. They need to be able to write according to a variety of structures—as essayist, journalist, correspondent, poet, or storyteller. Many children are able to convey their understandings and thoughts freely in writing, but for others it is much less natural and comfortable. Process writing strategies designed to encourage free expression are especially appropriate. Learning to communicate through writing is essential for each student to accomplish.

Yet another credible indication of youngsters' thought is their drawings. Lots of students like to represent their conceptualizations by illustrating a subject. Likewise, many of them find graphic portrayals produced by others to be particularly helpful to them in grasping the interrelationships of factors or events that make up the concept. Classic textbook depictions such as the trade triangle and the water cycle are examples of a graphic form that works well for lots of young adolescents who have more difficulty with the spoken or written word. Concept maps drawn by students also provide a graphic representation of perceptions, details, and interrelationships.

In the pedagogical literature, middle-level teachers are called on to create activities that are hands-on. In general, this expression refers to having students make or do by using their hands. Although such activities are generally valuable to learning as well as popular with students, it is the process of representing one's understanding in some kind of tangible form that is especially valuable as a process of integrating and relating ideas. Whether it is creating a working model of a volcano or designing a bulletin board that portrays American domestic life in the mid-18th century, students must think broadly and creatively and make discriminations to accomplish a coherent representation. Not only does such activity enhance learning, but it also provides evidence of thought that in turn enlightens the teacher as to the student's intellect.

Many of the same benefits of hands-on activities accrue when kids make presentations. Whether the presentations are serious original dramas, skits, simulations, role plays, or spontaneous interpretations, these revelations of knowledge and values reflect understanding, analysis, interpretation, organization, and synthesis. The essential ingredient here is that the presentations be original. One popular application of this insight is peer tutoring, in which the youngster doing the tutoring must understand, organize, interpret, and present the content to the child being tutored. Such situations provide teachers with a rich opportunity to gain insight into the tutor's intellectual development.

These processes of constructing understanding undergo a good deal of qualitative refinement during the multifaceted cognitive expansions of early adolescence. It is common for youngsters to struggle with abstract concepts, especially when the material being covered is conceptually beyond their grasp. They may feel failure due to their inability to understand, and they may withdraw from the struggle. Tragically, some become altogether alienated from formal school learning. If teachers avoid confronting students with material they're not ready to comprehend, certain failure at one point in time is prevented, and the possibility of eventual understanding is preserved.

The teachers who participated in this project worked at maintaining a deliberate attitude of responsiveness to children's revelations about their intellectual functioning and development. They created a variety of ways for their students to evidence growing sophistication in how they think—ever enhancing the capacity to think successfully and productively. These teachers made conscious, studied observations in order to recognize and support their kids' changes through tangible manifestations of thought such as those just described. Such evidence is often more subtle in a 12-year-old than in a 6-year-old, and thus it is easier to overlook unless intentional provisions are made to observe and document thought. This clinical attitude helps teachers to acquire the skills of alertness to clues and of well-organized documentation necessary to create well-matched learning activities.

There is, then, a sweeping but gradual transition in the ways youngsters think and process experience during these several years. There is not by any means a total metamorphosis in these years, but it appears that failure to move significantly and successfully from child-like thought to more adultlike thought in early adolescence has far-reaching and potentially long-lasting effects. Prudent teachers, parents, and other adult leaders attend conscientiously to their responsibility to cultivate youngsters' thought through experience. It is a goal of integrated study that students learn to think and act in ways that will allow them to solve the problems they face now and in the future.

THE CHALLENGE

From these four basic goals, clear directions emerged for the educational experiences we sought for ourselves and our students. Successful units could be assessed according to five observable criteria.

Students must succeed and must believe that they are successful. Every student wants to think of himself or herself as an effective, proficient, valued class member and learner, thereby growing in a sense of personal efficacy. We wanted the kids to experience the success, respect, and approval that generate the sense of personal worth they need and seek. We sought to create an expansive collection of diverse tasks that would increase the probability that every student would have a realistic opportunity to realize success. We resolved that their accomplishments would be acclaimed and rewarded.

Students must feel safe and secure. The fine line between discipline and freedom is realizable in a supportive context in which young adolescents are allowed reasonable limits that are open to negotiation. The interpersonal climate thus enhances or encumbers their school lives. In addition, physical restlessness can be accommodated by acknowledging its naturalness and by designing strategies that allow students to move around the classroom. We believed strongly that the moodiness we saw from time to time could be best handled by our being sensitive and positive and that we could inspire cooperation and loyalty by being simply nice to our students and supporting them. People who are simply nice to others inspire reciprocal expressions of loyalty and cooperation.

Students must have firsthand experience. By *firsthand*, we refer to learning experiences in which students are producers of knowledge. Students surveying a neighborhood for residents' opinions about a local issue is an example of firsthand experience; reading about someone else's survey is secondhand experience. Both types of experience are important to young adolescent learners, but less schooling time should be confined to classrooms and, therefore, to the secondhand exposure than is too often the only presence in middle grade classrooms.

Students must become the authorities of record about a subject by actively defining, generating, and organizing the experience that produces knowledge. More specifically, students need to come into direct contact with other people, events, and materials that are primary sources. They must subsequently create an organization by which to impart that experience as meaningful knowledge. The teacher's role is one of helping each student clarify his or her personal priorities. External standards must take the backseat to the timeliness of youngsters' deciding how a study is best ordered and reflected to others.

Students must work together. It is a truism that young adolescents agree to go to school because that is where their friends are. The social arrangement most alien to them is one that prohibits them from opportunities to talk with each other, to be in close physical proximity to friends, and to work and play together. This need for close peer contact is regularly in conflict with a school atmosphere that in its obsession with obedience imposes regimentation, silence, and isolation. Developments in grouping strategies within classes enable teachers to organize youngsters to better meet their need to be together in chosen groupings, which enhances their work ethic (Slavin, 1980; Johnson & Johnson, 1988). Students also need to learn from interaction with adults within and outside of school walls.

Students must become increasingly responsible for their own learning. An intimation of change in early adolescence occurs when youngsters more frequently and urgently express their need to be increasingly independent of adult values and ideas. They form their own perceptions about a host of personal life-style issues such as what clothes to wear and how late they can stay up at night. As adults know so well, it is not uncommon for youngsters' views to conflict with those of parents and teachers. This need for personal empowerment is often mistakenly perceived by adults as only rebelliousness. We must accommodate young adolescents' rapidly emerging desire to be more responsible by allowing them to do things they thoughtfully judge to be worthwhile and by fairly holding them accountable for their subsequent actions. In so doing, we help them explore their growing awareness of their emerging personal potential. We also affirm their ideas about how to improve the world we share.

A CLOSING COMMENT

Our challenge, then, was to move beyond merely an abstract and theoretical understanding of the implications of a curriculum based on young adolescents' needs. We needed to take some thoughtfully considered steps, creating designs that incorporated our best estimates of responsive, appropriate practice.

Having established a rationale based on our knowledge of kids and of topics of more likely interest to them than those traditionally prescribed, we devised planning frameworks and implementation processes. That work enabled us to define our projects in terms of content, organization, learning and teaching activities, and documentation. Having picked the tunes for this dance, we next turned to figuring out the steps! It was time to get on with it.

REFERENCES

Beane, J. A. (1990). *A Middle School Curriculum: From Rhetoric to Reality.* Columbus, OH: National Middle School Association.

Carnegie Corporation. (1989). *Turning Points: Preparing American Youth for the 21st Century.* Washington, DC: Carnegie Council on Adolescent Development.

Elkind, D. (1984). *All Grown Up and No Place to Go: Teenagers in Crisis.* Reading, MA: Addison-Wesley.

Erickson, E. (1968). *Identity, Youth and Crisis.* New York: Norton.

James, C. (1974). *Beyond Customs: An Educator's Journey.* New York: Agathon (Schocken).

Johnson, D., & Johnson, R. (1988). *Cooperation in the Classroom.* Minneapolis, MN: Interaction Books.

Lipsitz, J. (1977). *Growing Up Forgotten* (Report to the Ford Foundation). Lexington, MA: Lexington (D.C. Heath).

National Association of Secondary School Principals (NASSP) Council on Middle Level Education. (1985). *An Agenda for Excellence at the Middle Level.* Reston, VA: Author.

National Middle School Association (NMSA). (1982). *This We Believe.* Columbus, OH: Author.

Slavin, R. E. (1980). *Using Student Team Learning.* Baltimore, MD: Center for Research on Elementary and Middle Schools, Johns Hopkins University.

Chapter 2

Integrated Studies Planning Framework

Chris Stevenson and Judy F. Carr

As we began the work that resulted in the integrated studies reported in this book, we had the advantage of prior association with each other and some common beliefs and goals, as presented in the previous chapter. As our aim was to develop integrated studies, not discipline-specific, multidisciplinary, or interdisciplinary ones, we knew that our planning would be based on one all-important assumption: The physical, intellectual, social, and emotional characteristics and needs of young adolescents would provide the basis for all decision making. The countless curriculum guides we had encountered throughout our separate teaching careers, in which step-by-step objectives were content specific, was not a useful model for this endeavor. Because integrated studies are multidimensional, we needed a planning framework that acknowledged that complexity and provided a bridge from learner-centered goals to implementation of integrated, developmentally appropriate studies. Fortunately, there are a number of identifiable elements in the best of such studies, and these provided a framework with which our units could be designed.

CHOOSE A TOPIC

The focus or theme of integrated study should be inherently interesting to young adolescents. The teacher can choose, the students can choose, or everyone can agree on the choice of topic. However, the concept to be studied must generate genuine interest on the part of students so that the learning can be as authentic as possible. Bicycles, flight, the circus, early adolescence itself . . . the list is endless. The study of a river (see chapter 10) was based on student fascination and curiosity about the Winooski River, which bordered their school property. They fished in it, waded in it, threw stones in it, and related stories of their after-school adventures on its banks. The study of the roads of Starksboro, Vermont (see chapter 5), emerged because Mary Heins acknowledged her students' expressed interest in heavy equipment and machinery. As a result of such clues, marvelous integrated studies were developed. Along the way, students also happened to master a number of the more traditional teaching objectives articulated in their schools' curriculum guides for various disciplines. This result was an outcome rather than a starting point.

We began by listing everything we knew to be of interest to our own students. What did they talk about? What did they do outside of school? What were their hobbies and interests? What was going on in their world? Our preliminary list looked like this:

Music	Skiing	Baseball cards	Pets
Bicycles	Football	Clothes	Sports
Superstitions	Boys	Girls	Three-wheelers
TV	Dolls	Video games	Food
Money	Vacations	Rock stars	Movie stars
Movies	Themselves	Fads	Toys
UFOs	Collections	Photography	Superheroes

We also looked to our communities as rich sources of topics, adding some promising possibilities:

Cemeteries	Rivers	Lakes	Trucking
Mountains	Businesses	Services	Bridges
Dumps	Hospitals	Airports	Transportation
Careers	Power plants	Newspapers	Museums
TV stations	Malls	Barns	Radio stations
Fairs	Railroads	Churches	Local government
Circuses	Crafts/Crafters	Forests	Buildings
Roads	Farms	Senior citizen centers	

Believing that we teach best when we also feel some passion for a topic, each of us took into consideration our personal interests as we scanned these lists and worked toward final topic selection. The chapters that follow resulted from consideration of these initial brainstormed lists. Ultimately, the question each of us had to resolve was: Why choose this topic for these students in this setting?

IMAGINE POSSIBILITIES

Most topics can be studied from a variety of viewpoints. Ones that hold interest for particular young adolescents in a given setting lend themselves to virtually unlimited associations, connections, and possibilities. Rather than starting with the givens—What books do we have? What class periods are free? What are the objectives in the curriculum guides? How much money do we have?—we presumed to ask from the point of view of the young adolescent: What resources are out there? What activities come to mind? What could we do with the river? The dump? The mountain? The cemetery? How can we create knowledge? We engaged in open-ended, freewheeling brainstorming, which produced an abundance of unique, innovative ideas. We also had a great deal of fun together.

Having selected a topic, each individual or group constructed a web of activities, resources, connections, and materials that related in any way to the topic. Each individual or team working on a topic began the web by printing the topic in the center of a large sheet of chart paper and beginning a process of free association. Some groups chose to organize their webs by identifying at the outset categories that would organize the process. Some organized their webs according to disciplines (see Figure 2.1). Others chose to be guided by the nature and needs of young adolescents (see Figure 2.2). Others still chose not to risk limiting their imagination by establishing any categories at all.

As Peter Straub (see chapter 3) has often reminded us, "There is no such thing as a stolen idea." We used a collaborative process to develop fully our webs. First, each topic was explored by those of us who would eventually implement the study. When progress bogged down, we swapped webs with other individuals or groups and added to their webs, subsequently trading again until all groups had contributed ideas, resources, and connections to each other. We pumped each other's wells of knowledge and experience into a pool that overflowed with rich, exciting curriculum. This work at once drained and refreshed us, energizing us anew for our work. In any case, as the final web for the circus unit illustrates (chapter 12), the results were rich with possibilities (see Figure 2.3).

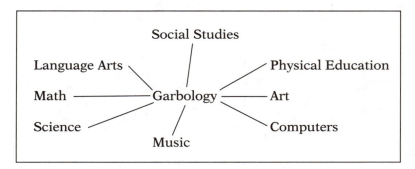

Figure 2.1. Discipline web.

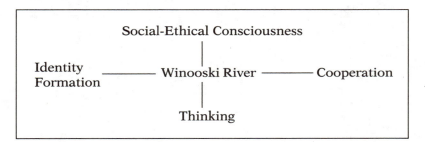

Figure 2.2. Young adolescent needs.

FOCUS ON A CULMINATING EVENT

From previous experience with integrated studies, we knew that such endeavors have a tendency to take on a life of their own. Identifying a culminating event at the outset helps to avoid what some of us referred to as the never-ending unit syndrome. Establishing a culmination ensures that the unit will in fact end, thus helping teacher and students to make the transition to other work that needs to be accomplished.

A culminating event also contributes focus to a study and enhances everyone's sense of accomplishment when it is completed. It not only gives students the opportunity to show off what they have learned, but it also builds class spirit and involves everyone—students, teachers, parents, and community members—in a shared celebration of learning. Students in the Big Alpha Circus unit presented their own circus in an evening performance for their parents, which was highly acclaimed (see chapter 12). Subsequently, they repeated selected acts at the closing session of the annual conference of the Vermont Associ-

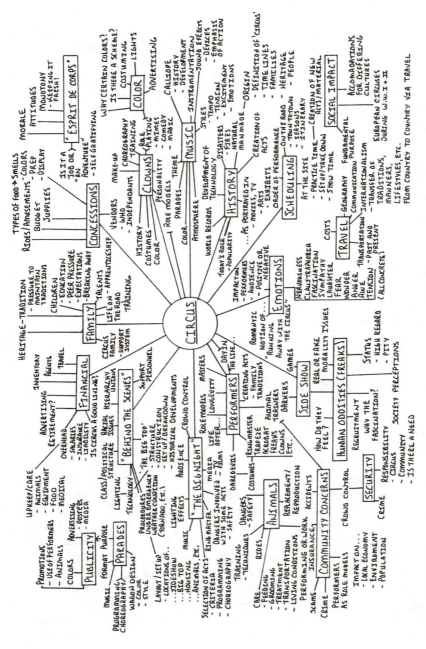

Figure 2.3. Circus web.

30

ation for Middle Level Education. Another example of culmination came after weeks of learning about many different aspects of the Winooski River: Students became part of the river during a challenging one-day canoeing adventure (see chapter 10). Open houses and fairs of various sorts are popular ways to bring integrated study to a close. Such events typically are of one of four types:

- *Performance*—a circus, reenactment, play, skit, musical, or documentary
- *Presentation*—to parents, community groups, political bodies, schoolmates, or younger or older children
- *Product*—videotape, slide presentation, art display, class book, newspaper, photography, or book
- *Outing*—field trip of hiking, canoeing, or camping

Culminating events need not be the only "big events" that take place during the life of the unit, however. Students involved in Climb Every Mountain began their study with a climb to the top of Mount Mansfield and ended with a presentation to parents (see chapter 11). Some students involved in the circus study spent a great deal of time at the Big Apple Circus during the summer and then performed their own Big Alpha Circus in the fall.

SELECT ACTIVITIES

Once the culminating event is identified, it guides the selection of activities that will take place throughout the unit. It is much easier to map the journey once the destination is determined!

Faced with the abundance of possibilities we had assembled on our webs, many of us struggled about what to discard and what to keep. We couldn't do everything. Believing that some activities and combinations of activities are, however, inherently preferable to others, we articulated the distinguishing characteristics of the preferred ones. These became both benchmarks and ground rules.

Provide Many Choices to Students

Insistence on greater student participation when deciding what is to be learned made good common sense to us. Ultimately, instruction was purposefully designed to create a balance between teacher-directed activities and student-directed activities. One organizational strategy that provides a balance of types of choices is to think of the study in terms of three options for students, also referred to as the Rule of Three (Stevenson, 1992, p. 154):

A. Activities about which students have no choice
B. Activities in which students make guided choices
C. Activities in which students exercise free choice

The first part, A, is composed of study and activities determined by the teacher in light of knowledge about what students need to learn and understand. Students are called on to trust the teacher's greater experience and wisdom in undertaking no-choice work. Part B is composed of controlled choices. Students choose from options offered by the teacher, who as a consequence of age and experience, knows valid, worthwhile possibilities for middle-level students. The third part, C, is an invitation to students to propose activities and devise plans that can be pursued through the school and its resources. The variety in this agenda incorporates learning that adults know their students need and at the same time acknowledges and addresses students' personal strengths and interests. By helping students learn how to choose well and then be successful in their chosen work while they are in the middle grades, we also help them practice for the more consequential choices of adulthood. Personal empowerment and self-confidence derive from our support of their curriculum choices.

Emphasize Problem-Solving Skill Applications

Young adolescents have myriad questions, fleeting curiosities, enduring interests, intuitive ideas, and biases. Deliberate exploration in a supportive home or school context can sustain and expand these learning possibilities. Two essential ingredients in integrated curriculum are opportunity and personal initiative. Children can gather a lot of the information they need to make sense of things by asking questions. As children advance through early adolescence, however, their questions progressively lend themselves to systematic inquiry. Finally, children need to make and present representations of what they have learned by such means as writing, drawing, constructing, photographing, graphing, performing, and sculpting. Showing what is learned is not limited only to writing, although few studies do not involve this basic craft. Displays, demonstrations, visual productions, and presentations to interested groups of peers and adults are excellent ways for students to convey original knowledge.

Thus, when young adolescents apply skills to solving problems, they explore, ask questions, and represent what they know. Consider the students in the Garbology study (see chapter 14). After personally exploring trash collection and garbage decomposition, they traveled to the local landfill. In the midst of a statewide solid-waste-management upheaval, they were encouraged to understand and to debate the issues they uncovered. They later represented their understandings using graphs, computer data bases, newspaper accounts, and other means.

In short, integrated studies begin with the bewilderment from which questions arise naturally. Based on such questions, a problem is defined and a process is undertaken through which these questions can be explored and resolutions can be proposed.

Use the Community as a Resource and Laboratory

The importance of the involvement of adults from outside the classroom cannot be overstated. Parents, neighbors, and other community members all play roles as teachers in integrated studies. Students especially use community experts as important primary sources of information when exploring issues and seeking to answer questions of personal interest. Students involved in the A View From the Park unit not only identified community members who could provide needed information, but they also made their own appointments to meet with those individuals (see chapter 7).

Integrated studies also provide students with opportunities to engage in service relationships with their communities through work in existing adult service organizations, homes for the handicapped and elderly, and elementary schools. Such out-of-class involvement is vital to integrated study. Whether students are interacting with home, neighborhood, or community, going on the road to travel, or using the U.S. mail, rich resources are available outside of our schools and are waiting to share with them. Taking advantage of those resources makes learning come alive.

Provide Firsthand Experience

Middle-grade students learn best when they work with primary sources of information to develop their own knowledge and skills. Thus, real-world experiences, problems, and issues are provided, simulated, or duplicated in integrated studies. Rather than reading about what is involved in running a business, each student in the Adopt a Business unit spent a half-day internship in the business that was under study (see chapter 8). Prior to seeing a movie about the impact of pollution, students taking part in the Garbology unit built their own minidumps for collecting, categorizing, and weighing their own family's garbage. Subsequently, they prepared and presented a report on garbage accrual for decision makers in their town (see chapter 14). The learning that results from these sorts of experiences is learning that will last a lifetime.

Complement a Variety of Learning Styles and Modes in a Balanced Approach

A wide variety of activities demanding an assortment of skills ensures that every student can be involved and successful. The Winooski River study, for example, offered more than 25 separate activities, ranging from reading a book about the Winooski River to taking the final 9-mile canoe trip adventure.

It is particularly important to remember that growing children need to move around. The changing distribution of body fat around an enlarging, expanding skeletal system makes sitting in hard chairs extremely uncomfortable for many youngsters. Some emerging evidence also suggests that the attention span of young adolescents when hearing a lecture or recitation by another person averages around 7 minutes. These students function best when they are provided with a variety of instructional modes and seating arrangements. In short, activities that involve reading, writing, listening, and speaking should be balanced at least in equal measure by ones that involve doing.

Encourage In-Depth Study

By spending a significant amount of time on one theme, students at this stage of development can satisfy their intense need to become good at something. They become engrossed in learning details and truly understanding the subtleties of a topic. Students learn a lot as they immerse themselves in the study. This is in stark contrast to students whose teacher covers merely a lot of facts or simply assigns additional homework or pages to read to provide depth. For instance, the students in the Adopt a Business study found out all they could about a local small business (see chapter 8). To become experts on that business, they had to learn at many different levels, a reality that had a positive impact on their self-esteem. In essence, interaction with adults in the business world compelled students to raise the level of their attentiveness and understanding. Community members who attended the culminating event spoke enthusiastically and publicly about the quality of the children's work. One proclaimed, "This is what the future of curriculum in the middle grades needs to be!"

An in-depth study also takes on a life of its own. Students and others bring in new ideas and questions that stimulate continued exploration and learning. Questions often continue long after the study has ended. Even several months later, new questions may be raised by students. As one team that participated in this work commented, "We tried to end it, but the children kept finding new connections." Although this may complicate scheduling and planning from a traditional teaching point of view, many teachable moments are realized that would otherwise be missed. Furthermore, such continued student interest is certain evidence of authentic learning.

IMPLEMENT THE STUDY

At last it is time to begin! Three additional caveats apply to the actual implementation of the study.

Use Students' Questions to Direct the Planning

Students' questions are the heart of integrated study. "I'd like to learn more about freeze-dried foods." "How high is Mount Mansfield anyway?" "How did that statue come to be in the center of the village green?" "When am I going to grow taller?" Such questions lead to the "found" curriculum, to topics that are right in front of us but are often overlooked. Once the topic of study is identified, students' questions about it expand and sharpen the study's focus.

Students in the river study worked in cooperative groups to develop a concept map to show what directions they wanted the study to take (see chapter 10). They also put together their final unit test, filling it with questions much more difficult than those their teacher might have asked. Yet they all scored very well.

Teacher preplanning is essential prior to implementation of a study, but student contributions to planning are equally crucial. Each study should begin with student participation in brainstorming about topics and identifying possibilities, questions, and connections in ways similar to those already conducted by their teachers. Student-developed webs can be very useful for pre-assessment, often adding new directions and focus and frequently identifying additional resources for a study. Parent and community experts can be identified in this way: "My neighbor is a mortician." "My uncle is a stone carver." "I know a quarry we could visit." In fact, young adolescent students can also handle much if not most of the responsibility for the logistics of the study: sending letters, making phone calls, creating work schedules, designing and printing invitations, and assessing their own work and that of their classmates. It is through such student contributions that a study comes to life and becomes owned by the class.

Employ a Variety of Grouping Strategies

The size of small working groups within a class or team changes throughout the study, depending on the nature of a particular activity. Various structures—the whole class, a small group, and an individual—are employed throughout the study. In addition, decisions about how kids are grouped are made according to their interests and choices, not some so-called measure of ability. At times groupings are based on interests, at times on needs, and at times on choices. Cooperation is emphasized because both the study and individual students benefit from each other's contributions. Competition is not only unnecessary; it is antithetical to integrated studies.

Stress Student Accountability and Responsibility

As student accountability and responsibility increase, student involvement and interest rise proportionately. Young adolescents are capable of being much more accountable for themselves and their learning than educators usually expect. Keeping accounts means creating structures and guiding students in maintaining records of their activities, studies, and decisions—and then holding them accountable according to the structure. Students in the river study kept daily journals of their activities (see chapter 10). Knowing how much time has been invested and which activities were carried out in relation to a task clarifies circumstances for the student (and teacher). Responsibility for educational progress then rests squarely where it belongs: shared between students and teachers. In addition, it is urgent that we create conditions in which young adolescents may organize time according to sequenced work plans that they develop themselves. For instance, the Adopt a Business students made their own appointments with local businesses (see chapter 8). By maintaining documentation files, journals, and self-assessment accounts written every few weeks, students become much more accountable for their school lives and ultimately more fully responsible for themselves.

DOCUMENT AND PUBLICIZE THE STUDY

To render students' expressions of regret (e.g., "I wish—", "If only I—") unnecessary, teachers should document as many aspects of a unit as practical, initiate a publicity campaign, and see that students articulate what they are doing and learning. Some unobtrusive ways to do this that both contributed to documentation and enhanced student learning were incorporated into these studies.

Pictures, slides, and videotapes, as well as photocopies of selected student drawings and writings (with students' permission, of course), should be made regularly for use in a variety of ways. This task need not be overwhelming if students take responsibility for it. An inexpensive camera loaded at all times with film and kept in a central location in the classroom ensures that promising photo opportunities aren't missed.

Articles in newsletters, the local paper, and local, state, and national professional publications, as well as regular updates for parents and colleagues, can be written by students and the teacher to inform all concerned about what is going on.

Curriculum connections can be articulated and shared with colleagues. Although integrated studies do not use formal curriculum expectations as their starting point, the reality is that they can often address more of the required objectives in meaningful contexts than is the case with more traditional deductive, prescriptive approaches. It is important to make sure that parents and other teachers understand that this is the case.

Finally, a calendar of all activities that will take place during the study, along with selected invitations to parents, colleagues, administrators, and community members, can be an important public relations tool. Thus, outside participants experience firsthand the legitimacy of integrated studies.

ASSESS AND EVALUATE STUDENT EXPERIENCE AND LEARNING USING A VARIETY OF TECHNIQUES

The best assessment tools are valuable teaching and learning experiences. Authentic assessment is limited only by the imagination of the teacher and students. Folders, journals, presentations, videotapes, letters, drawings, models, and student-generated tests—all provide valid means for students to demonstrate learning. Assessment in integrated studies is intended to discover what students have learned in the broadest sense possible, rather than determine only that they have or have not learned a particular body of content, skills, and concepts predetermined by the teacher. Thus, the question becomes: What have students learned about X? rather than the traditional orientation reflected in: Do students know 1, 2, and 3 about X?

Evaluation differs from assessment in one essential regard: criteria used. Adults seem to know intuitively the difference between grades of A and C. Yet there is an urgent need for kids to understand the criteria by which teachers establish standards and reflect differences in the quality of academic work. They need not be confused by why and how grades are determined. A sure way to avoid such confusion is to involve them in the processes of establishing explicit criteria and examples for critiquing their own work. When equivalence is stated between a numerical score and a letter grade, students can interpret their work easily. However, because much of the work appropriate for them to do in integrated and other studies is subjective, the potential for confusion is increased. Sadly, teachers all too often avoid evaluating what is inherently subjective knowledge by testing only material that lends itself to objective testing. Most of the material tested by standardized tests exemplifies this practice. Consequently, teachers committed to empowering their students through integrated studies can engage them by helping them to establish standards by which they can evaluate their own work. Clearly explained and demonstrated criteria substantially reduce anxiety and confusion about evaluation. Furthermore, such criteria show kids that high standards are realistic and accessible. To evaluate student learning without these criteria overlooks a perfectly timely opportunity.

EVALUATE THE STUDY

Once the study has ended, it is worthwhile to take the time to determine how successful it has been. Questionnaires completed by students and participating community experts and parents, focused discussions with teammates, and review of teacher and student journal entries all provide valuable information that can be used to redesign the study in the future. Therefore, it is important before implementing the unit to identify what is to be achieved by it. For one team whose integrated study is included in this book, a key issue was how well they would work together as a team during their first joint effort. Another teacher was interested in which learning activities his students found most helpful. No matter what the evaluation focus, it is important that it be undertaken soon after the study is completed.

This planning framework and these steps have served us well in planning the studies described in the following chapters. We believe that each of these studies gives ample evidence of intellectual engagement and learning that are plainly and positively authentic. Therein lies the artistry of teaching.

REFERENCES

Stevenson, C. (1992). *Teaching Ten to Fourteen Year Olds*. White Plains, NY: Longman.

STUDIES OF SELF

Chapter 3

The Big HooHa: Toward Sound Mind and Body

Peter Straub

Mount Abraham Union Junior High School, Bristol

What do skipping rope, practicing slow breathing, Ben Johnson, oat groats, yoga, taking pulses, listening to a university soccer coach, and "Dear Oma" letters have in common? Had that question been posed to my seventh graders in the beginning of September, they would have said, "Huh? I don't know!" Ask them now, and they'll say, "Plenty!" Why the change?

How did seemingly disparate parts become elements of a study? It's simple: Just mix equal portions of seventh graders' needs with a teacher's desire for exploration—then heat with serendipity. What resulted from this recipe was, for us, a wonderful excursion into motivation and health.

As with any good integrated study, this unit was designed from the outset around selected students' needs that reflect their physical, emotional, and social changes as the primary focus. This unit was to focus on the need for personal excellence and to resolve to work for it. To learn this, children must come to understand their particular talents and capacities for controlling their lives:

1. I can directly influence the health of both my body and my mental well-being.
2. I can work out solutions to problems that don't have a single right answer.
3. I have special skills, and I can do things that make me a valuable member of a group.
4. I can help others to be successful.

These statements became the underpinnings of the goals and structure of Toward Sound Mind and Body.

The cornerstone of our unit was having the kids experience personal improvement and success, as well as having them get a feel for what it takes for that success. Writers like Erik Erikson (1968) and Charity James (1974) have clearly established that children in this age group need experiences that allow them to develop their identities, to feel success, and to develop a sense of self-worth. These are perhaps the most important needs that children have.

In addition to students' needs, a teacher's personal needs and professional responsibilities should also be incorporated into an integrated study. I had a need to break out of the mold of teaching kids science. My district labels me a science teacher, yet I have always thought of myself as a kid teacher. In that light, my career has been spent searching for ways to reach and teach my students *through* science, but I had never really broken away from teaching *science*. Designing an integrated study based primarily on adolescent needs provided just that opportunity.

So that any outcomes of the unit could be assessed, it was essential that goals were articulated. Kids need to be able to do the following:

1. Judge and assess themselves as compared with themselves, not others. They need to start to establish elements of a personal vision for excellence and success.
2. Plan, implement, and document programs that will allow for their own physical improvement (they have direct influence over their physical well-being).
3. Work supportively within and between groups (teams), as well as with each other as individuals.
4. Gather useful information regarding Sound Mind and Body through a variety of means, such as interviews, inquiries, speakers, and field trips.
5. Help plan, organize, and run the culminating Olympic event: the Big HooHa.

So that we would have a tour guide to prevent aimless wandering in our journey, student activities were created. The students would engage in the following activities:

1. Develop a plan for training, and train for an individual event for the Big HooHa Games. To win in the games, one must show the most personal improvement.
2. Measure and record individual pulse and weight changes over a month's time, and maintain graphs for each.
3. Explore ways to reduce pulse rate, such as systematic training, experimentation, and biofeedback.
4. Attend a variety of talks by guest speakers from the surrounding community on topics relating to health, heroes, and self-improvement. Speakers will include physicians, coaches, dentists, organic gardeners, people who had lost much weight, and aerobics/fitness instructors.
5. Support Mr. Straub in October on the Birthday Marathon Attempt.
6. Reflect through journal writing on experiences and class discussions.
7. Participate in the Big HooHa Games, part I, both as athletes, teammates, and spectators. Participate in the Mini-HooHa Games, which will be spread over the rest of the year.
8. Design posters to communicate a key concept of the unit.

Because I was breaking new personal ground and setting aside some established habits, at times the whole unit felt like doing acrobatics on a trapeze without a safety net. However, like the safe completion of a maneuver on the trapeze, the successful completion of this unit gave an exhilaration that was unlike any other I have felt in my 16 years of teaching.

Armed with these goals and ideas for activities, I took some deep breaths and prepared for the opening of school. Knowing this experience would create its own twists, turns, and opportunities that I could not anticipate, one of the difficult things to do was to communicate clearly to my colleagues and department chair *exactly* what was going to happen. From what I had heard from others who have done integrated studies, this could only be accurately done *in retrospect*. ('Tis true!) After giving my general description and a "Trust me!" to those who needed to know, off we went.

My personal journal entry of August 29, 1988, reads, "[This unit] will test my real teaching skill. Perhaps a subtitle for me *ought* to be

'Working Without a Net.'" In preparing my room for the kids' arrival, instead of putting up preestablished lists, information, and answer keys, I created areas for the kids' input and lists like the Important Word List, Who Can We Contact List, and Things to Find Out About List, as well as the I Now Know/I Think That Box for inquiry information. Whenever words came up that any of us thought were important to understand, they were added to the Important Word List. The Who Can We Contact List was generated through class discussion and suggestions from the kids' parents. As names were suggested, they were added to the list. This served as our basis for contacting potential speakers. The I Now Know/I Think That Box collected index cards on which the kids recorded what they learned or what they thought about various questions and queries that I would put to them. It served as our inquiry collection center.

Knowing that our unit would be a bit different from what the kids were used to, I felt it appropriate to begin by using an analogy. The upcoming month was likened to my two years of building an addition onto my home. To successfully build it required a dream, many ideas, research, learning, hard physical labor, frustrations, and a lot of help from friends. Our unit would contain many of these same elements. The kids felt that if things were tightly planned and always worked out as expected, it would be a less exciting experience. (This quality is great for an integrated study, but I don't recommend it for an addition to your house.)

To start them thinking about what it means to be successful, one of our first activities was to make definitions of what it means to achieve in class. Their definitions included, among others, to succeed at a goal you have set and worked on, to accomplish, to carry out something to a successful end, to set high standards and reach personal goals, to do the best you can compared with yourself, to conquer goals, to master something, to try and learn, to try your best, to make progress, and to achieve something you haven't been able to do in the past. Having them write their definitions not only had them thinking about a concept we were to pursue, but it also gave me insight into their thoughts. We were ready to begin.

Two current articles about adolescent health and fitness gave us food for thought. They were not read to answer preestablished comprehension questions, but rather as a stimulus for the kids to ask questions about their fitness and health. Our sights were aimed at personal physical improvement.

To aid in our investigation, we generated a list of community members who might speak to us about their perspectives on health, fitness, and/or success. Those who were invited and spoke to us were two teachers in our school who together had lost in excess of 180 pounds, an herbalist, an organic gardener, a university soccer coach, a dentist, and a doctor. We also started to take our pulse and weigh in on a regular basis, graphing these data over a month. In our junior high school, any gathering of the entire student body for the purpose of fun, such as games, lip-sync contests, and plays, had become known over the years as a *HooHa*. Thus, I established the Big HooHa as a central feature of this unit. In a nutshell, the HooHa is an event composed of a multitude of games in which each student takes part in one individual event. Pretraining performances were established during the first HooHa. These performances set the stage for the month-long training that was to follow. Integral to the training were the development and pursuit of a plan that would help the HooHa athlete to improve over the course of the month. You see, winners would be determined not by who was the best, but by who *improved the most!* To prevent sandbagging, the kids were informed of this *after* the first HooHa. They responded very favorably to the idea. Everyone had a chance to win!

Unit activities were well under way by the 2nd week, with guest speakers coming in, training occurring on days permitted by the weather, and pulses and weights being tracked. As we can always expect the unexpected, it was no surprise that serendipity affected us in a number of ways:

1. We observed from the daily data that some kids' pulses were going up, the opposite of what was desired. After talking about possible reasons for this trend, we concluded that many kids were not relaxed when they took their pulse. They were encouraged to lie down for 2 to 4 minutes on gym mats in the room before they took their pulse. We also practiced some yoga. Over the month, their average pulse rates declined eight beats per minute. The kids found that *they* could influence their heart beat!

2. Kids found out that what they wore caused 2- to 4-pound fluctuations in their weight, especially when they wore those popular jean jackets. This was a perfect opportunity to teach the concept of experimental control and the importance of precise measurement.

3. Part of the information we were given by our organic gardening guest speaker concerned the amount of sugar that is added to cereals. (Check the boxes in *your* cupboard.) An inquiry showed that as a group, the average sugar content of our cereals was approximately 16%. Sixty-nine percent of the kids expressed the view that this result

was either "quite good" or "great"; they didn't think the evidence would cause them to alter their cereal-eating habits very much.

4. The Ben Johnson steroid affair occurred during our unit. What was bad for Ben was a great opportunity for us to delve into our own values. Discussion led to an inquiry that not only let the kids in on what was potentially dangerous about steroid use, but also something about the pressures put on people to win. To help us explore this issue further, each kid went home and talked over this question with his or her parents: Assuming Ben Johnson was guilty of steroid use, what was wrong with it? The responses they brought back to class were:

21: He broke the rules; using steroids is cheating.
16: Using steroids gave him an unfair advantage.
13: He was doing damage to himself and his body.
5: He just wanted to *win*, not necessarily do *his* best.
3: It was wrong because of the punishment he received.
2: He wasn't really doing his *own* best.
1: He was a hero and a role model who was teaching bad habits.

These results were then given to the kids as choices from which to pick the *two* that they felt were the most severe. They responded:

27%: He was doing damage to himself and his body.
25%: He was a hero and a role model who was teaching bad habits.
17%: Using steroids gave him an unfair advantage.
11%: He broke the rules; using steroids is cheating.
11%: He wasn't really doing his *own* best.
9%: He just wanted to *win*, not necessarily do *his* best.
0%: It was wrong because of the punishment he received.

These returns enabled the kids to see what each other believed. They also gave me some intriguing glimmers of insight into the moral reasoning of my students—a topic to pursue at another time.

5. In listening to a cassette tape put together by a friend, I ran across a song called "It Takes a Whole Lotta Help to Make It on Your Own," by Steve Forbert (ASCAP, Actual Music, 1982). I first listened to this tune near the end of the unit, close to the time I was to attempt a marathon run on my birthday, an event I dubbed the Birthday Marathon Attempt. Besides giving us the chance to enjoy an upbeat, fun song, the lyrics gave us the opportunity to brainstorm ways that we could positively affect our performance. This became a spark for

emphasizing the effects we have on others and their performance, too. It helped us focus our minds on helping each other.

The 5 weeks had gone well, but the kids were now ready for the culminating event. We were guest speakered, graphed, measured, journaled, inquired, and trained out. In planning the unit over the summer, I had decided to attempt to run a 26.2-mile marathon on my 37th birthday as a personal celebration and as a concrete example of what personal goal setting and achievement were all about. It turned out to be just that and more. The kids and I measured and laid out my marathon course around the school grounds. It would be 20 laps of a 1.3-mile loop. As the run was to occur during normal class time, each class was responsible for recording my loop times and monitoring how much liquid I drank as well as providing me with emotional support. An added bonus was that no substitute teacher was available while I ran, so they *had to* perform their duties on their own.

The marathon day was cold and windy, and a bit of snow was in the air. The kids' enthusiasm and participation warmed me, however. They performed their parts magnificently, making sure my liquids were ready, turning the lap cards to let me keep track of how far I'd run, recording the times, and giving me encouraging comments and cheers as I passed the support table. Many also ran and biked portions of the loops to keep me company. The emotional lift they gave me on the last two loops, when our whole team was out there cheering their hearts out, touched me very deeply. It also allowed me to finish well. I'll never forget the end as I stood stooped over with my hands on my knees, glad to be done. The kids surrounded me, cheering and patting me on the back. We shared the pride; they had played a part in my achieving my goal, exemplifying how "It Takes a Whole Lotta Help to Make It on Your Own."

The final major event was the Big HooHa—the 17 uncommon events designed to show kids that if they do indeed work at something, they can improve. Although the events themselves may be incidental, our emphasis was on the relationship between effort and improvement. The results, shown in Table 3.1, clearly illustrate the validity of the concept.

The Big HooHa results couldn't have been much better. Kids who had been really conscientious about their training had done very well, showing marked improvement. The question now was: Have the kids realized the unit goals?

To assess this, they were given two final tasks: First, they were to construct a poster that, to them, represented an important idea or con-

TABLE 3.1. Results of the Big HooHa Event

Event	Average Improvement (%)
Card Toss	140
Watermelon Seed Spit	118
1 Foot Balance	100
Tennis Ball Flight	94
Upside-down Pull Ups	51
Schmerltz Toss	37
Jump Rope	28
4 Minute Lap	28
Coordination Test	24
Wrong Armed Throw	24
1 Foot Hop	18
Backwards Spring	17
Rubberband Shoot	12
Shuttle Run	9
Stair Sprint	8
Standing Long Jump	6

Summary: 68 participants at final "test"
59 improved (87% success)
9 did not
Average Improvement Overall = 62%

cept from our month-long unit. Second, they were to write a Dear Oma letter (*oma* means grandmother in German; I called my grandmother Oma) telling what the most interesting, important, and memorable things were in the unit and why they chose them. To ease the strain of writing, a skeleton letter was provided to allow their thoughts to flow. They copied it over in their own hands. These two inquiry assessment tools gave me the information I needed to see if the month's journey had given kids what I had hoped.

Once attached to the walls, the posters showed the wide variety of experiences and ideas we had pursued during the unit. It was very pleasing to see the variety as well as the kids' unique perspectives and ways to communicate what they felt was important. From this measure alone, it appeared that our goals had been realized.

The Dear Oma letters added even more evidence that the kids had internalized what the message, both stated and implied, had been. Referring to the unit goals, their responses are summarized as follows:

1. The students will judge and assess themselves as compared with themselves, not others. They will establish and articulate elements of a vision for personal excellence and success.
   - *Favorite things:*
     My favorite thing was that everyone was a winner.   2
   - *Most important idea of the unit:*
     In order to improve, it takes effort and practice.
       I improved!   17
     We need a good attitude (belief in ourselves).   13
   - *I will remember:*
     The HooHa results.   13
     Improvement takes effort.   5
     We must have self-confidence.   2
     Fitness is important.   1

2. The students need to understand how to plan, implement, and document programs that will allow for their own physical improvement. (They have direct influence over their physical well-being.)
   - *Favorite things:*
     Training for the HooHa.   21
     Measuring and graphing.   9
     The yoga.   2
   - *Most important idea of the unit:*
     It is important to keep fit; what we do now will
       affect us later in life.   10
     Taking our pulse and weight daily.   7
     Setting small daily goals helps us feel successful.   2
   - *I will remember:*
     Practice really works!   5
     Training for the HooHa.   4
     The Ben Johnson affair.   4
     Doing the graphs and measurements.   3

3. The students need to understand how to work supportively within and between groups and teams, as well as with each other as individuals.
   - *Most important thing about this unit:*
     It takes a whole lotta help to make it on your own.   5
     Helping with the marathon.   5

- *I will remember:*
  It takes a whole lotta help to make it on your own.   2

4. The kids need to understand how to go about gathering useful information regarding Sound Mind and Body through a variety of means, such as interviews, inquiries, speakers, and field trips.
   - *Favorite thing:*
     The guest speakers.   11
     Nutrition information.   1
   - *Most important thing about this unit:*
     We need good nutrition.   4
   - *I will remember:*
     The talks on nutrition.   4

5. They need to understand how to help plan, organize, and run the culminating Olympic event: the Big HooHa.
   - *Favorite thing:*
     The Big HooHa.   21
     The Old Man Marathon.   8
   - *I will remember:*
     The Old Man Marathon.   17
     The Big HooHa.   13

Well, we were done. From the assessment done through inquiry, it was evident that my goals had been achieved. The kids told me of our success in a vibrancy that left me in an excited state for days! It was also time to identify curricular and basic competency objectives that we had addressed during the unit, even though curriculum per se was not the primary focus. We touched on the following areas:

Measurement
(time, weight, and height)
Graphing (bar and line)
Scientific method
Nutrition
Letter writing
Listening
Drugs
Analysis

Health
The cardiovascular system
Percent
Averaging
Computation
Proofreading
Design and drawing
Interpersonal skills
Act 51 (Vermont drug and
alcohol curriculum)

It was intriguing to see that although a decision to teach kids rather than science had been made, the kids had many opportunities to learn a great deal about science and its skills throughout the unit.

One of my personal goals had been for this unit to act as a springboard to other units during the rest of the year. Work has been done now for mini-HooHas (no pun intended) to be included in most of the human body system units, and a problem-solving fair, the Invention Convention, has been established, allowing it to become the basis for a Chapter 2 mini-grant award.

The success of Toward Sound Mind and Body stimulated me to dream and plan for its refinement and improvement. Plans are already afoot for modification and integration of Toward Sound Mind and Body into the English and math classes for next year, including field trips, a wider variety of speakers, personal success posters, learning how to dissect a task into component parts, and an awards/parents night. Now we must be careful not to let this unit expand to such a degree that too much of next year is taken up by it.

I hope that the excitement this unit generated in my kids and me is obvious to the reader. It was successful because every day was vital and fresh—not only to them but also to me.

When we asked if the unit ought to be run again next year, the delay in their response was only a micro-second: YES! It must be that success and improvement make kids feel good! What they may not realize is that it is continuing right now in subtle ways and that it will continue for the rest of the year if not beyond.

REFERENCES

Erikson, E. (1968). *Identity, Youth and Crisis.* New York: Norton.
James, C. (1974). *Beyond Customs: An Educator's Journey.* New York: Agathon (Schocken).

Chapter 4

A Self-Study

Janet Bellavance and Susan Girardin
Camel's Hump Middle School, Richmond

> Their Way
> The longest journey
> is the journey inwards
> Of him who has chosen his destiny
> Who has started upon his quest
> For the source of his being. . . .
> *Dag Hammarskjold*

Who Am I?

To my peers I am:	another face, name, a person to challenge, someone to pick on, a girlfriend, someone to honor, someone to ignore, someone strange.
To my teachers I am:	a grade, name, face, number, questioner.
To my parents I am:	a child, a teenager, a responsibility, a slave.
To me I am:	me.

Kristin (eighth grader)

What had started out as a unit about the systems of the human body evolved into a much more comprehensive study of ourselves. Our combination class of sixth, seventh, and eighth graders wanted more. They wanted to know about sexuality, about different beliefs in our culture, and about each other. Simply presenting the unit in traditional ways—"Here are the systems of your body, and here's how they work"—was no longer possible. Our kids wanted to know it all: everything about the development they were experiencing at the moment. They looked at themselves as people with unique histories, potential, strengths and weaknesses, emotions, and ideas. It was their curiosity and readiness for introspection that would shape our study in the coming weeks.

As teachers we had our own goals. Knowing that our students were working to sort through physical and social changes that they were experiencing, we wanted to help them clarify "Who am I?" in terms of roles, relationships, values, and physical selves. Given their inate curiosity about their bodies, we also wanted them to understand the physical changes they were experiencing. Knowing how their bodies develop, change, and work would enable them to make informed decisions about their health. Social interaction is paramount at this age; therefore, it was important to have kids identify their interpersonal values. Hearing each other talk about their beliefs and struggling to clarify their own values gave students a better understanding of how to make decisions in the face of social pressures.

At our middle school, the two of us teach in an alternative multiage program that we designed to provide increased opportunity for interdisciplinary teaching and learning. Our philosophy is strongly built on making connections between disciplines and showing the inherent relevance of what is being taught. We chose to create this particular unit knowing how well the material would lend itself to an interdisciplinary study. Rather than teaching a unit that focused exclusively on scientific content, we were able to build our reading, writing, health, and guidance curricula around the theme of self-study. We divided the study into four sections entitled To Be or Not to Be (identity issues), Nuts and Bolts (anatomy), Birds and Bees (sexuality and reproduction), and A Mind of My Own (mental development and the brain). Our text was a collection of information and resources that we had gathered from a wide variety of sources. Each student received a three-ring binder to contain the notes, personal journals, handouts, and other literature they'd accumulate during the study.

We knew that parents should know about this unit ahead of time because of its personal nature and the discussions we hoped would occur at home. It was important to us that parents became involved in the parent-child-related issues we expected to study. To that end, we sent parents a letter that described the different parts of the unit and the topics we expected to cover. Within the letter was a section in which parents could give feedback in the form of materials to recommend or share, other resources or services they could offer, and their ideas or questions about any aspect of the unit that might concern them. The letter also established a foundation for communication and support that we were able to draw on throughout the weeks to come. The majority of parent responses were supportive and enthusiastic. A wealth of materials came in, including suggestions for speakers and for topics to explore and offers to assist us. As we anticipated, the topic that concerned parents most was sexuality. Parents' questions were well founded and led to some good discussions with them.

In the first week of the study, we learned what these adolescents had on their mind as they each created a newspaper about themselves. Students titled their own newspapers and wrote an editorial, a letter to a "Dear Abby" column to which another student responded, a comic strip, a poem, an advertisement aimed at adolescents, and an essay in which predictions for the future were made. Once again, we were reminded how much students—even six, seventh, and eighth graders— like to cut and paste, draw, and design. Although each student produced his or her own paper, the layout aspect of the activity enabled students to sit together, talk with each other, and share the ideas they were incorporating into their papers.

Students revealed sides of themselves that gave us insight into how they perceived themselves. Jill showed us how important it was to her to be part of the group; her poem let us see a Jill who otherwise might not have been recognized in this way.

Just Like Them

They always seem to think,
If there's an A,
It's mine.
I never wanted them to think,
That I'm always right.
I just want them to know,
That at heart,
I'm really just like them.
They seem to always think,
If there's one who likes to study,
It's me.
I never led them to believe this,
They just assumed it on their own.
I'd just like to tell them,
I'm really just like them.

Jill

Once students began talking and writing about their inner thoughts, they found it more difficult to separate who they were and wanted to be from who society appeared to define them as. We started looking at images of adolescents in the media. We saw ads that showed the right kind of jeans to buy, the only kind of snack food to eat, and the latest music to listen to. From these images and messages, we brainstormed what the adolescent culture is: Adolescents like to take risks, like to be with their friends, enjoy snacking, are concerned with their appearance and with being part of the group, and spend a lot of time watching television and listening to music. We looked at how the media portrays adolescents. Advertisements stressed beauty (perfection), boy-girl relationships, body image (weight, size, and height), and convenience (snack foods).

With this new awareness about advertisers' techniques, students created their own commercials advertising a fictional product aimed at adolescents. It was clear that they were experts at selling what appeals to them. Video Day was filled with laughter. Critiquing one another's commercials helped them become more aware of the media's influence on them.

Using this contrast between who they are and how society defines them, students read short stories dealing with identity issues and responded to them in their journals. We were struck by the students' candor. It seemed that after having created, talked, and laughed together, an easier, more comfortable trust was being established. There was rapport that seemed to give permission for us to talk to one another about the size of our noses or feet, pimples, jealousy of siblings, anger, feelings of exclusion, and longing to belong.

After reading the poem "Richard Corey," students wrote about what others see them as and what they really are:

> Because I wear glasses they think I'm a nerd or a goody-goody. They also think I'm super smart and all I do is study. Just because I do all my homework and get good grades doesn't mean I'm a goody-goody. Even though I don't look it, I like rock music.
>
> *Norma Jean*

> They think I'm snotty because I'm shy. I'm completely different than everyone else thinks. I'm not snotty but I'm shy.
>
> *Jeff*

> I'm concerned about people finding out all the things I hide because they scare me. I'm afraid I wouldn't be liked.
>
> *Will*

After reading Cher's biography, in which she talks about how she came to understand herself, students wrote about the changes they would make about themselves:

I hate my nose. I wish it was smaller.
Adam

I would like to change the world and my sister.
Ben

I wish I could change the size of my bones. Everyone thinks I'm fat because I have big bones.
Jennifer

We observed that none of our students were entirely happy with themselves as they were. But what was important for us as teachers to discuss with them was that change is natural and healthy. It's a necessary part of growing. And as important as change is, it's also important for growth and development to accept who we are.

The self-study then took an unexpected turn. We couldn't talk about what we wanted to change about ourselves without talking about what was most important to us: our values. As a class, we looked at the different stages of moral development as explained by Lawrence Kohlberg and how moral codes affect our ideas and behavior. As an initial exercise to increase student awareness of the different values we hold, we gave them some hypothetical situations to react to. Students got into intense discussions about the range of responses to the following hypothetical situation: You are in the checkout line in a store about to pay for four albums when you realize the cashier has made a mistake and has rung up only three of them. What do you do?

1. *Tell her and pay up. Because:*
   It's the right thing to do.
   It's not right to steal.
   It's not right to rip off the store.
   I wouldn't want to be in her shoes (I feel sorry for her).
   I don't want to get the cashier in trouble.
   I'll get respect from her.
   I can't lie.
   Maybe I'll get a discount or reward.
2. *Don't say anything! Because:*
   You'll get more for your money.
   It all evens out (K mart charges more than Zayre).
   It's her mistake, not yours.

It depends on her attitude (nice = tell, mean = don't tell).
It depends on if she's new at the job.
It depends on her title (a manager should be smarter).
I'd give her a second chance.

We also spent a lot of time making distinctions between big decisions and moral dilemmas. Deciding whether to go to college is a big
decision. Deciding whether to sneak into the movie without paying is
a moral dilemma. Some students were able to see the difference
clearly, while others had difficulty grasping the distinctions. Their
confusion made us more aware of differences in how our young adolescents comprehend and think. For some of our students at this time
in their lives, a moral dilemma was still an abstraction they were
unable to separate from ordinary decisions. Several students wrote in
their journals about personal moral dilemmas, why this question was
a moral dilemma, what choices were available, and what their decision
was. This was another time when we could glimpse the issues and situations our young adolescents were struggling with, how they
thought, and what their bases for decision making were. Some students were very concrete about their opinions of right and wrong,
while others were able to have their own opinion but still see more of
the gray areas:

> I had to decide whether or not to tell my mother about this party a
> friend was having. I knew if I told her about it she wouldn't let me go
> and I really wanted to go. I didn't want to lie to her because I know
> she trusts me. I decided to tell her I was just going over to my friend's
> house. I didn't feel very good about my decision.

As a follow-up exercise, each student was given a list of moral
dilemmas. The hypothetical situations included finding a wallet with
money and identification in it, entering a room when people are talking negatively about a person you like, discovering that your co-
worker/friend has been overcharging customers and pocketing the difference, not being able to afford the medicine that will cure a loved one
of a fatal disease, and having to evaluate a partner/friend on a group
project when he or she has done very little of the work. Each adolescent
chose a situation; interviewed an adult, a peer, and a younger child; and
wrote down their various responses. Many students were surprised to
see the difference in the reasons that motivated the three people to
make their decision, even though all three may have made the same
choice. This exercise helped to make the students more aware of their
own values in comparison with those of others.

Until this point in the study, kids had done a lot of talking, writing, and role playing. We created a bulletin board to provide a visual representation of each of the three aspects of development we were studying: physical, intellectual, and moral. Kids were asked to bring in a representation of each category. The following day, the bulletin board was covered with items such as report cards, jump ropes, pieces of baby blankets, and "stop killing the seals" bumper stickers. Students put their items into one of the three categories. We could see their growing understanding of these dimensions of their development.

It was obvious that our students were eager to begin the reproduction and sexuality section of our self-study. We were somewhat apprehensive, however. Would we be able to answer their questions? Would we be embarrassed? How would we handle the inevitable snickering? How much should we tell them?

We began with brainstorming all the possible things any of the kids could want to know about sexuality. For over an hour, we listed our questions:

How is sperm made?
How do Siamese twins happen?
What is a good age to reproduce?
Do boys have anything like a girl's period?
Why do I like girls all of a sudden? I didn't use to.
Do your insides get bigger as you get larger?
What happens if a baby is born too early?
Why do girls have babies and boys can't?
How do the sperm and the egg find each other?
Why is it so hard to talk about sex?
How many times does intercourse occur before a baby is made?

Seventy-five questions were typed, copied, and distributed for students to add to their notebooks. For the first 20 minutes, we sat in a circle for informal discussion. With many reference books around us and with the knowledge that we'd probably need to follow up our discussion with questions for some experts, we tried to deal responsibly with every question. This routine turned out to be a wonderful way to ease into each class because it laid a foundation of caring and support. We were able to discuss using appropriate language, we learned how to avoid hurtful laughter and inappropriate remarks, and we demonstrated how we could be sensitive to one another's questions and responses.

Question 17: How do you know if your body is making any sperm?

WILL: You don't know. It happens when it happens. That's why you never know if a baby will be made.

MATT: Yes, you do know. My brother told me that it happens as soon as you have puberty.

MARTHA: As soon as a boy is 14, he makes sperm.

MATT: Honestly, it's the waiting and what goes on in your head. Like whether or not you're the only boy in the class who can make sperm. There's sure a lot of big talking in the locker room!

Throughout the unit, kids wrote in their journals about questions concerning sexuality. We encouraged them to share answers in group, but no one was ever required to do so. From time to time, our reactions to their writing pushed them to think further.

Question 6: What's the hardest part of going through puberty?

NIKI: The hardest part is the way parts of my body are growing. My big brothers pick on me as if I can stop what's happening.

TIM: I want to have more control over what I do, but I don't know how to do it without fighting. I think it's puberty that is making me feel this way. It's real hard.

GENEVIEVE: Waiting around for my period is difficult for me. Maybe if I wait until I'm 22, it won't be so hard on me. I'm scared to tell my mother when I do start.

EMILY: I feel itchy. Itchy all over. My mom says it's because I'm almost a teenager. Is that good or bad? Nothing fits me anymore—my clothes, my desk chair, or my skin!

A particularly interesting guest speaker was the pregnant mother of one of our students. The kids had lots of questions about pregnancy for her to address. She was forthright in her responses to questions about morning sickness, the birthing process, pain, her limitations and expectations, and the "what ifs" the kids asked. When her baby arrived shortly after her visit, they all made a huge card with cutouts showing Nathan (the newborn) in all stages of his development.

These students had begun to acquire debating skills from studies earlier in the year. When questions came up about whose responsibility it was to provide kids with sex education, we decided to debate the issue. After the kids wrote personal viewpoints in their journals, we organized them into small groups to talk about their ideas:

CHRIS: Kids shouldn't put so much responsibility on their parents.
They have enough to worry about. Let the teachers do it.

JENNY: He's right. Besides, my parents won't tell me anything. I have
to ask my sister, and I think she's making up a lot of stuff.

COLBY: You're lucky. My parents tell me more than I want to know.
Teachers have had more practice with sex talks. They should do it.

ADAM: Even though sex is a secret everyone knows, I don't want to
have everyone hearing about my body. I would get nervous.

JENNY: I want to learn about it with my friends. That way, we'll all
know the same things, not just bus stuff.

One debate was not enough. In fact, as students talked with their
parents and gathered more information, they wanted to pursue the
issue. These times were, indeed, teachable moments! We supported
their need to share their conjectures about the numbers of children
they'd have; whether they would have children (all said yes!); their children's names; and what, how, and when they'd tell their children about
sexuality. Then they each wrote a letter as a parent to their fictional
children. Bobby wrote to his daughter, Ariel, especially poignantly.
After having warmly told her about having her period, he then wrote:

> Now Ariel, I know you might be thinking what a scary thing this is and
> how you'll feel really weird. But, I'll be there for you to help you
> through it. It'll be worth it because then you'll be a woman (even if
> you'll always be my special girl).

We spent three weeks studying other systems of the body: digestive,
respiratory, central nervous, circulatory, skeletal, and reproductive.
Students conducted labs and wrote and taught mini-lessons to each
other. They used art to demonstrate how each system worked. An especially fun learning experience to help them digest all this new information was called Body Games. Kids worked in small groups over a 2-
week period to design a game about one system of the body and how it
works. The game had to review the major organs, show how the system
functioned, and show how it was related to other body systems. The
design of the game had to be worked out by each group.

As a class, we brainstormed games that students liked to play and
what it was about them that made them fun: choices within the game,
risk-taking opportunities, challenging but not too difficult skill level,
variety within the game, and chance. Each small group submitted a
design plan and conferenced with one of us before constructing the
game. Game formats included board games, "trivial pursuits," televi-

sion quiz shows, games with contestants, and a life-size maze that the students actually traveled through. Some groups made elaborate props, prizes, and costumes. Each group wrote a handbook for their game, which gave the title, directions, and rules of the game. In the end, we exchanged games, and students played and evaluated other groups' games.

Again, the journals were windows into their thoughts: what they were feeling, how much they were learning, and what they were concerned about. The game activity was instructional, but it also had deeper roots in showing them how to work in a small group. The activity enhanced group participation, and it also helped us to show the different roles in group work. Students took turns in the roles of recorder, observer, and facilitator while they all practiced listening to and encouraging others. Some of the journal comments about what went on during the game construction were negative, but they provided fruit for some great discussions about what works well, who you work with best, what kind of comments are especially helpful, how to make suggestions, and so on.

KENDRA: I learned that I like to be the boss and will always tell people what I believe or want.

KELLY: Groups that work together well don't always come up with the best ideas.

ANDY: It's easier to work in a group. You always have someone who will do the hard work and you always have someone who will fool around.

PETER: I would rather work with people I chose than with a group I'm assigned to. When I'm assigned a group, I don't want to cooperate with them. I feel trapped and I sort of rebel. I will work hard if I choose my partners.

BRAD: I wish we had exchanged games before the final day so that we could find out ahead of time what was confusing with ours and get the bugs out.

Speaker Day was the culminating activity, designed to tie together all of our experiences and help answer some of our accumulation of questions. Students and teachers helped identify professionals from every walk of the health community: a nutritionist, a counselor, a physical therapist, a doctor, an athletic trainer, a social worker, a midwife, an acupuncturist, the Red Cross, an AIDS worker, a drug abuse counselor, and someone to talk about adoption. Volunteer students contacted the workshop leaders to get background information to introduce them. The students collected whatever equipment or materials the speakers needed and met them at the door with a friendly smile. All students chose to attend whichever specific workshops they were most interested in. Four 45-minute sessions were scheduled to run throughout the day. As teachers, we felt that Speaker Day was a responsible, informative way for kids to explore their interests in more depth and in smaller groups. It was also fun. We asked kids for their reactions to the workshops:

JUDY: I thought the whole workshop was wonderful because I'm adopted. I learned how a family is affected by infertility and adoption. The group was really into listening to that mother's story.

TOM: I really like the experiments with blood pressure and heart rates that we did in one of the workshops I went to.

CINDY: My best workshop was one where I saw a movie showing a birth. It showed what they really had to go through.

TIM: Dr. F. did a good job talking about AIDS. My mom thought so, too. I didn't know very much about it, but now I do.

JILL: I liked the adoption one. I think it took a lot of guts to stand up and talk like that. I liked the story of her life and how she tried to have a baby. She adopted, but it took a long time. It was sad because it was true.

ADAM: I liked when the sports trainer showed us how to tape using Ira's ankle. It was funny.

Following this successful Speaker Day, we asked our students to evaluate the past 6 weeks. They responded to three questions:

What did you learn about yourself?
I work good in groups.
I like writing private things.
I don't like a lot of things about myself.
I knew more about sex than I thought I knew.
I have good parts and bad parts.
I'm going through a lot of changes and I need to be more patient.

What did you learn about other people?
Girls go through a lot more things within their bodies than boys do.
None of us is alone in our thoughts and feelings.
Some kids who were jerks can be great friends.

A lot of things that people say happen to our bodies aren't true.

What was your favorite part of the unit?
We had a lot of choice about what we wanted to do and how to
    work.
Moral development. I'm really interested in how people think.
Making the commercial for our product.
Body games. I liked being in a group because it was fun designing
    games.
We learned the systems in a fun way.
We didn't just do one thing; there were a lot of activities.

Using these data, we returned to our goals to see if we had accomplished what we set out to do. Our primary purpose had been to have our students become aware of and understand the many changes they were experiencing. In order to fully gauge our success, we had to look at measures other than test scores. Students' journals, parents' letters and participation, community response, and our own informal discussions with one another and our students were our evaluative tools.

One student's initial journal response seemed to illustrate what we were trying to accomplish:

> On the inside I'm really a pretty neat person. It's too hard to explain,
> but my insides don't always approve of what I do on the outside.
>
> *Ben*

We hope that through the self-study, Ben and his classmates learned to understand and listen to their inside selves.

COMMUNITY STUDIES

Chapter 5

On the Road Again

Mary Heins
Robinson School, Starksboro

Choosing a topic for an integrated study that would interest my particular class was especially challenging. My class consisted of 26 students, the majority boys. I knew the dynamics of this class had caused undue headaches for teachers during the previous 5 years. I'd seen power struggles over academic work and in social interactions. I knew that in order to make this unit work, I needed to grab the interest of every single one of my students. I also knew they had to experience this unit and connect it with their interests.

Our school is located in a rural farming and bedroom community about 20 miles south of Burlington, Vermont. The school has 130 students in grades 1 through 6; each classroom is self-contained, with one class for each grade. The students who enter my classroom come in with abilities that have a wide range, with varying socioeconomic backgrounds, and with values that are immense in their differences. I wanted my students to find and make positive connections between themselves and our small community.

My class also needed to be able to work in a group situation. Their apparent inability to interact positively and comfortably with each other was a major concern. They needed to learn to listen and to respect each other's opinions, to participate actively in activities, and to share their thoughts. I also wanted them to simply feel better about themselves as learners and as people. These individuals needed to view their own talents and ideas positively. Having them participate in decisions that would be made about this unit would be the first step in our work toward those goals.

ROLLING RIGHT ALONG: GETTING STARTED

"Tell me all you know about our town roads here in Starksboro" was my opening statement as I began to plan this unit. The diversity of their responses was encouraging:

> Route 116 is paved.
> There are lots of cars.
> There are less cars on dirt.
> Plows angle and knock over mailboxes.
> It is fun to ride bikes, three-wheelers, and horses and to walk there.
> It is icy, has frost heaves, is rough, has mud holes, is snowy, has holes, and has bumps.
> It has bridges.
> There are buildings.
> It needs repair.
> On dirt roads, grass always grows close.
> Some buses can't go on them.
> It is dangerous.
> There are rules and signs on roads.
> It used to be cobblestoned.
> Many roads are dirt with loose stones.
> There are lots of accidents, especially with animals.
> Different roads have different speeds.
> We have lots of dirt ones.
> Routes 116 and 17 are the main ones and more traveled.
> State workers and town crew work on them.
> They are useful.

Right away, it was evident that the topic engaged them. Every student contributed at least one response.

Next, I asked, "What would you like to know about our town roads?" These were their questions:

Why isn't my road treated like a paved one?
What equipment do they have at the town sheds?
Who are the crew, and how much are they paid?
Do more people work in the winter than the summer?
Who is our road commissioner?
What is a road commissioner?
How many students live on paved roads versus dirt roads?
Why does the road always repair in pieces?
How do they repair bridges, culverts, and potholes?
What is pavement/tar made of?
How do they make a road?
Where do they get salt and sand?
What are the pros and cons of road salt?
How are roads named?
How were the roads taken care of 50, 75, and 100 years ago?

These questions became the basis of our study.

Next, students were asked to locate their houses on a town map. Journal entries written directly following this activity illustrate a range of levels of student thinking:

> I found my house on the map; it was easy. I would like to spend a day with the town crew. I also want to visit the Shelburne Museum and the town shed.
>
> *Seth*

> I made a picture of my house in a circle. I couldn't find my house on the map because I didn't know where I lived on the map.
>
> *Craig*

> For the last hour we drew pictures of our houses. Some people colored and some people outlined their pictures. We taped the pictures somewhere next to a town map and attached them to a piece of yarn. The yarn stretched to the place on the map where we live.
>
> *Damon*

After this activity, I felt that connections to our community were really beginning to happen. Finally!

BUMPY ROADS AHEAD

Starksboro has 43 roads, not including the 2 state roads that run through our town. Only four of these roads are paved. Before I began this unit, I had visited the town offices and had obtained a list of roads and a general highway map of the Town of Starksboro. Each road had been given a number and a name. I made flash cards using the road names and organized the students into small groups to work with the cards. They were to find the roads on which their school bus traveled.

> Today we took cards with the names of the roads in Starksboro and grouped them to match our three bus routes. We don't know all the roads.
>
> *Amy*

> We learned what roads we pass on our way to school and home. I learned the name of two new roads.
>
> *Dylan*

Many of the students spent time with their individual town maps and a list of roads. They were interested in the names as they went to and from school. They were excited to find out exactly where their fellow students lived! Typical of their comments were:

> I thought you lived closer, Seth!
> How come the school bus doesn't travel up Little Ireland Road?
>   Carl lives up there. It should.

These discoveries led to an explanation and discussion about the classification system established for roads. Here is a quote from Jonathan's daily journal:

> We put the roads in Starksboro in classes. Class 1 roads are taken care of by the state and are in good condition. Some are Rt. 116 and Rt. 17. Class 2 roads are aided by the state and are in O.K. condition. The other roads are Classes 3 & 4. Some are Tatro Road and Hillsboro Road.

Jonathan's journal showed his understanding not only of the four classes but also of the differences between state roads and town roads. Several discussions were held concerning the assigned number, class, and condition of the roads. As students sorted, categorized, observed, and described, they were demonstrating how capable they were of systematic thinking.

CROSSROADS

Three very important community members provided the students with useful information. Our local historian, Bertha Hanson, showed us slides of old houses along our roads. Many students recognized either their own house or a neighbor's house. These houses dated back over 100 years, so the condition of a particular road was of interest to all. Entries from a few journals follow:

Bertha Hanson came and showed us slides of Starksboro 100 years ago. I learned what Starksboro was like. The town had a church and meeting place and the roads were small and thin. Also they spelled Starksboro a longer way. Starksbourgh. I liked it because it was interesting.

Dylan

We saw the school on a slide when it was only one room.

Annette

I learned about my house a little. I think it was fun because I learned a lot of history.

Adair

The roads were like sidewalks. Jolene's house used to have a porch on the second floor but they took it off. It was weird and neat. It was like you went back in time and were really there. Some kids said that it would be awesome. Some of the people used horse-n-buggy and some used old cars.

Karin

Bill Coon, one of our town's selectmen, visited us, too. Before he came, we brainstormed interview questions. He also brought along newspapers and catalogs that specialized in road equipment. Through the interview, many of the students began to feel a personal connection to our town and to adults in our community.

Amy's journal included:

Thursday Bill Coon came into our classroom. We learned about a lot of things that I don't think we would have learned without him. I learned what size salt comes in and that in the winter time they can't always use salt because it freezes, so they use sand.

YOU TAKE THE HIGH ROAD, I'LL TAKE THE LOW ROAD

Many of our activities were done in groups. Large town maps were used to estimate and then measure precisely the length of many of our roads. We were interested in finding out how many miles of road we had in Starksboro. During this activity, I wanted each student to contribute his or her own ideas. Students also needed to encourage others to participate and needed to support others. Most kids had very little difficulty in staying on the task. One group in particular enjoyed working together, and they produced high-quality work. On the other hand, I had one student who realized and admitted very honestly that he "was not a group player." At this point I talked with him, emphasizing that although we may not all be group players, there are times when group participation is necessary.

The students were beginning to formulate many questions concerning our town crew and the equipment they used. I then contacted our road foreman, Bobby Briggs, and arranged for a field trip to the town sheds. I, myself, knew only that they were located near the town dump. The students prepared interview questions for him and were anxious to see what equipment they might find there. Here are a few journal entries about our trip:

We went to the Town Sheds Friday. We saw the Traxcavator, tractors, and other equipment. We got some samples of rock salt, cold tar, fine sand, and gravel.

Craig

We saw a gigantic cliff of sand, rock, and boulders. Next we saw the salt pile. When we got back to school we took the samples we had collected and made a display and chart.

Damon

The road crew gets up at 2 AM to check the roads in the winter.

Angie

We saw the new equipment used to fill in muddy roads; the fabric looked like a roll of carpet. Bill Coon said that they bury it in the road and it soaks up water. My road now has fabric to stop the mud in the spring.

Amy

The experience of visiting the town sheds was exciting to everyone. Many of the students climbed into the trucks and all over the grader. They formulated questions for our foreman, who explained the specific skills needed to run the double auger and the grader and how they "put up the winter sand." Many realized for the first time the vital importance of our road crew to our community.

CLEAR SIGNS AND FEW DETOURS

One final project consisted of a roadography, a report on a specific road. Not surprisingly, many chose the road where they reside. Information included in this report classified the road as a 1, 2, 3, or 4 road; gave its length in miles; described the surface; estimated the number of houses; and pointed out cemeteries and interesting places of business. All the students decided to sketch their road on oak tag, adding actual dwellings along the road.

Another final project involved drawing road equipment seen or read about in the past few weeks. The equipment sketches decorated the hallways of our school for weeks. They included dump trucks, graders, plows, the town sheds, an old horse-drawn grader, and a snow roller seen at the Shelburne Museum. These pictures were also on display during our annual Starksboro town meeting in March, and parents and townspeople could see the results of our study of town roads. Town meetings in Vermont are occasions when townspeople have their chance to speak about issues that are important to them as taxpayers. The roads have always been a subject discussed with strong feeling. Comments usually range from the cost of a new truck to the improvements of the culverts on class 3 roads. My students felt that they had acquired an understanding of a subject that concerned the adult world.

A NEVER-ENDING JOURNEY

My classroom faces Route 116, the main road through our town, and all winter long my students noticed whenever a green-and-yellow town truck or an orange state truck passed by. Some students also revealed their continuing interest by asking their parents which roads were discussed at the town meeting. It was clear to me that students had a new awareness of and interest in Starksboro.

Four students lived on roads on which a new fabric had been installed as an experiment the previous summer. The fabric was supposed to improve roads during Vermont's mud season, usually in March and early April. Their interest in the unit was revived when the snow and frost began to melt and mud season was upon us. Our local paper published an article about the new fabric roads, and one of the students brought it in to class to share. Here are a few comments I heard:

I remember seeing that stuff at the town sheds.
I know where that road is.
My road certainly is better because they put the fabric on the
    road.

END OF THE ROAD

An integrated study is a student learning activity that involves skills and content from several academic areas. Many units are planned jointly by a team of teachers, but my team just happened to include only my students and myself. Planning and developing this unit with my class gave students an ownership that they had never before experienced at school. They developed working relationships with their peers while working in a group, and they met community members and enjoyed learning about their community's past history. These interactions formed positive connections for them that enabled them to feel better about themselves. In their 6th year as a class, they finally demonstrated that they could cooperate and work well together. Choosing a topic of interest, engaging them in the process of planning the unit, and selecting high interest, personally relevant activities were the key to their success—and mine, too.

Chapter 6

Richmond Four Corners

Susan Girardin
Camel's Hump Middle School, Richmond

I designed this study about our community to begin my first year of teaching in an alternative program that our school created to provide greater opportunities for teaching interdisciplinary curricula. I wanted my first unit to accomplish several goals all at once. Because the program and the students were so new, I needed something to start the year off with a bang—something that would grab everyone's attention and help build good relationships among students and between them and me. The subject of community study was already a part of the science curriculum, and I began to see possibilities for enlarging it into an integrated study.

A community is a collection of people working together for a common good. Couldn't this be the focus, then, of our new program, as well as the small town where we lived? Our class was a community. Class meetings, a morning sharing time, and decision making together would help build a strong foundation for trust, respect, and friendships later on. The very nature of the young adolescents I was to teach determined how things would be structured, how material would be learned, and how we would grow together. A curriculum rich with opportunities to practice decision making and independent thinking seemed essential to students' individual success and the program's success.

Learning about communities in science and practicing and growing within our classroom community were good ideas, but I still needed to find a way to make the idea of communities relevant and important to these kids in a broader, even more concrete way. That's when I remembered a study another teacher had done with his students about their town. We could do a similar study of our town, Richmond, with a major focus on its single intersection, where as one of my students put it, "You have to go through to get anywhere in the world." All of their reading, writing, social studies, and art and some mathematics could be incorporated into this one study, making it truly interdisciplinary.

To help these kids learn to work together and lean on one another's expertise, part of the study would be organized around small-group work and projects done with a partner. As it was also important for me to get a good idea of each student's skills, part of the study needed to be conducted on an individual basis. I came up with a sketchy idea of what I wanted my class to learn and then presented the idea to the students, asking for their input in designing the rest of the study.

Lots of their ideas seemed to fit into large categories: schools, fire and police departments, and skiing (two ski areas are located nearby). Others showed more individual preference, such as a particular business or company. We organized our study as follows:

Part I:	Study of Richmond businesses (done by individual students)	2 weeks
Part II:	Community issues and problems (done with a chosen partner)	2 weeks
Part III:	Richmond study (done in small groups selected by teacher)	1 week

Part of my initial responsibility was to identify available resources. I sent a letter home to parents that described the upcoming study and requested materials and suggestions. Parents' replies were supportive of the study as well as filled with a wealth of information. Parents sent books, pictures, names of people who might be guest presenters, and offers to chaperone field trips into town. One parent suggested that after the study was completed, it would be a good idea to compile it and have it published. We could sell the booklet and make some money for the class. I brought up the idea at a class meeting, where it was discussed (I should say "chewed over" because the process was so new to students). The class agreed that the idea was sound and that they were willing to work hard to achieve it. The money we might earn was voted to go toward a 2-day trip to a winter environmental camp. Their faces radiated their pride, and excitement to begin the study was infectious. This study was becoming *their* project, and *they* wanted it to be successful.

We wrote a letter to the local paper describing our plans and inquiring about the possibility of visiting their office soon. The kids also thought it would be a good idea to include a rough schedule of when we would be downtown and who we would be visiting. These emerging adolescents were eager to take on a great deal of responsibility very early in the study. They felt what they were doing was important, and they were determined to see it through.

Before beginning part I, we talked at length about evaluation. I asked students how we could keep track of what everyone was doing as well as how well it was being done. Together we determined what would get passed in for grading, where editing would be done, how we'd conduct ourselves in public (as Jen said, "our image"), and that conferences between them and me at the end of each part would be an important part of the evaluation. Satisfied that there wouldn't be any surprises, these eager kids got started.

We brainstormed all the local businesses we could think of to begin part I, the study of Richmond businesses. Each child wrote his or her first three choices of businesses that interested them in their journals and described why they were interesting. This gave me a chance to understand their ideas and priorities before assigning each of them a business to study in depth.

> I really want to adopt the hardware store. My Dad goes in there a lot but we never have time to hang around and ask questions about the place. I've been thinking that it would be a neat place to work for when I'm in high school. I like how it smells.
>
> *Trevor*

We then listed lots of questions and selected those that interested us most. Role-playing with each other, the kids rehearsed how they would ask their proprietors for an interview and a tour and would arrange a time and demonstrated how to be courteous and understanding.

While downtown, we also made some preliminary pencil sketches of each business being studied and of the Four Corners area of town. As this was our first outing—especially to talk to the host businesses—

the kids were jittery. Certain elements of this initial contact were beyond my control, and I felt it necessary to talk with the class about some possible negative responses and how to handle them if they should occur. Most requests for interviews were quickly granted, adding to the children's growing confidence in the project and themselves. They had discovered that people were generally kind and considerate, that no one would bite their heads off if they made a mistake, and that they weren't going to be laughed at. In fact, some of our merchant's efforts were applauded, as Cathy wrote in her journal:

> Mr. L. was so nice to me. He made me feel important, like I was another businessman. He even thanked me for coming!!!

Back at school, we talked about the interview process, the necessity of courtesy, the importance of getting the facts, and how to look for less obvious changes in the interviewee, such as changes in voice inflection, facial expressions, and attitude toward the interview. Again students rehearsed with one another, making note of the ever present "But what if . . . ?" "But what if I drop my pencil?" "But what if I ask a question and it comes out backwards?"

These were legitimate concerns, not to be ignored. We discussed each issue and came up with viable solutions in the event that such "catastrophes" occurred. It seemed especially important at this time for me to be supportive and patient with students.

I spent additional time discussing with the resource teachers and Title I teachers how to help our shared students participate in the study. Using tape recorders and a shorter list of questions, these kids were also able to conduct successful interviews and share the pride everyone felt.

> I met Betsy at the Daily Bread Bakery. She was carrying in some groceries. I thought then that I was going to screw everything all up. We sat down. The bakery was noisy with a lot of people talking all at once. There was no place to plug in my tape recorder (Betsy thought it ran by batteries), so we went into the kitchen. It was busy in there but it sure smelled good.
>
> *Steve*

Because the interviewing process was lengthy and involved, we spent an entire week downtown before part II came into play. With partners of their choice, students had to identify a town problem or issue that they wanted to learn more about. The kids were also hoping that if research about these issues was publicized, perhaps the town would take some action to deal with them. After the problems or issues were identified, a field study and a survey were conducted. Some of the issues chosen were Richmond's zoning, the availability of parking, shopping preferences, garbage collection, and public signs. Partners met with me every other day to confer about their plans and progress. Preliminary sketches and diagrams were made as we waited for other students to return from their host businesses.

After the initial interviews were completed, the students and I discussed what went well and what didn't and how they could improve what they said and did. It was about this time that I noticed just how far we had come and what we had accomplished in so short a time. Genuine concern for one another was increasingly evident in how we discussed the interviews. Students who hadn't really said much in class meetings or during class were now opening up and showing some trust. They had grown in their confidence that no one was going to laugh at them or put them down as they described what their interviews were like. I think this happened so quickly because they owned what they were doing, they were in control, and it was their study. It is such an important issue to young adolescents to feel as if they belong to something important that is greater than themselves.

Their journal entries at this time provided further evidence that we were on the right track.

> I thought Mrs. Kipp would think I sounded dumb, that I would be not important to her. I thought she'd send me away, but she treated me like an adult.
>
> *Norma*

> The bank lady Jane talked real fast. She smiled a lot, especially when the vault alarm went off accidently. For a minute I thought I set it off! I wasn't the only one who was nervous—lots of kids were.
>
> *Darren*

> In my opinion, he was sort of shy and although he was funny, he didn't seem really comfortable talking to me. That's not what I expected. It made me feel great!
>
> *Cathy*

> This book is really going to be something! Everyone's doing so good with their interviews. I hope mine sounds as good as everybody else's.
>
> *Trevor*

When I sat down to do my interview the chair rolled backward
into some keys, knocking them on the floor. I was embarrassed.
What a way to start! Darren said the bank alarm went off while he was
there. I didn't know that Darren was nervous too.

Paul

A lot of these initial experiences and impressions were good introductions for their drafts. I encouraged students to tell these anecdotes in their writings because they were a good place to start and made for interesting reading. After conferencing and editing, a second draft was typed on the word processor and saved. We mailed these drafts to the respective businesses with a cover letter explaining how corrections, deletions, or additions could be easily made and were encouraged. We asked them to contact us for approval before the final typing. Some proprietors even wrote back to us (see Figure 6.1).

It's worthwhile to mention at this point that this study certainly promoted further communication with our town's residents. People in our community and my students shared goodwill that would be beneficial to us all in the future. Everyone had benefited from our work thus far.

Meanwhile, the partner projects that composed part II were well under way. Some students elected to find out more about their issue by arranging meetings with people directly involved with it. For example, one pair met with a town lister, who is responsible for assessing property values, and the town clerk to learn all about Richmond's zoning regulations and land use policies, which the students subsequently represented with a graphic of their own design (see Figure 6.2). Two other boys went on the town's garbage truck route after school to get answers to their questions. Another duo working on parking issues spent an afternoon with one of the partner's uncles who is handicapped. His wheelchair prevented him from gaining access to several businesses. He helped the kids see firsthand how Richmond could provide better parking. Once they had accumulated as much information as they needed, they completed their diagrams and put together their "man on the street" surveys to discover what Richmondites thought about their issue.

Once again we traipsed downtown. By now we were recognized by lots of townspeople, who would stop to inquire about this phase of the study, ask when they could get their copy of the booklet, and wish us well. Our confidence continued to grow as our support system broadened. The kids found out that surveying was fun, but we had too many surveyors and not enough surveyees! Everyone cooperated and gave enough information for my students to compile some data.

Dear Steven,

I enjoyed our interview and your write-up of it. You caught me saying some funny things!

The Four Corners project sounds very interesting. I look forward to seeing the completed project.

Perhaps you all would like to choose a few pieces from the project to send in to The Richmond Times. The Nov. deadline is Friday Nov. 7. We would love to share your work with the whole community.

There were just a few corrections.

Thanks,

Betsy Bott

Dear Gibson:

I am in receipt of your letter of October 8, 1986 with an attached interview. A review of the interview leads me to believe that you did a very good job with the interview and with your subsequent report of the interview. You paid attention to details and reported them accurately.

However, I would like to make two comments which should lead to corrections. In the first paragraph you, said I had a slight beard. I really do not have a beard and would prefer that deleted. In the second paragraph, fourth sentence, you used the word "seen" and I believe you meant to use the word "seem". I am sure this is just a typo.

I enjoyed our interview and hope you keep up the good work.

Sincerely yours,

David M. Sunshine, Esq.

DMS:bv

Figure 6.1. Letter from Betsy Bott, proprietor of the Daily Bread Bakery *(top)*; and David Sunshine, attorney-at-law *(bottom)*.

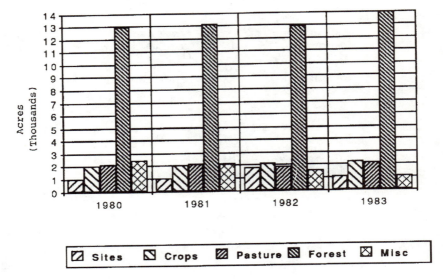

Figure 6.2. Richmond land use.

Gib, Paul, and Trevor canvassed the people of Richmond to find out why people chose to live in Richmond. Their field study included looking at people's homes and inquiring about real estate pricing, development, and availability of land:

> During our survey of people living in Richmond, we found that most people liked their town and enjoyed living here. People really didn't want to change too much about it either. About sixty percent of the people we interviewed on the streets of Richmond have lived in this community for twenty years or more. On a scale of one to ten, people generally rated Richmond an eight and a half. People plan to continue living in this town because they enjoy their lives here.

Part III of the study was centered around broader topics concerning Richmond. I organized small groups of four and five students to ensure a good balance of skill levels. The children chose to research the following: Richmond's Round Church, Four Season Sports, the police and fire departments, and the educational backgrounds of people living in Richmond. A requirement for their part III study was to create ways other than writing to present information that they uncovered in their research and to arrange for a guest speaker to come to class.

These young adolescents had done a great deal of public speaking by now and were accustomed to approaching townspeople and asking for help. It was a little more difficult, however, to be specific about what they wanted from their guest and what they hoped the audience would learn from them.

> I called four people before someone said they would come in to talk to us. It was harder being patient this time but I'm glad I stuck it out. My group couldn't believe I finally got him. Mr. Cochran (a well-known ski area operator) will be great!
>
> *Christine*

One guest speaker representing the historic Round Church brought in a large folder of pictures of old Richmond. The kids loved going through them, comparing the old pictures with the current pictures. We were invited down to the church the following day for a tour. Kids in that group felt accomplishment in that they had managed not only to invite in a guest but had arranged a field trip, too. The superintendent of our school district and our building principal were invited to answer lots of questions about school policies such as snow days, school hours required, how teachers were hired, and how supplies were paid for.

> Mr. Boyden (Superintendent) really knew our school. I couldn't believe that it cost $3,500 for each kid every year and that my parents pay most of this in taxes!
>
> *Jennifer*

> Mrs. Shroeder told us about the flood of 1927. The bridge I live near was blown away!! I wonder if my Grandpa remembers the flood. When I see him this weekend I'll ask.
>
> *Mike*

One group decided to present their research about historical Richmond in diary form. Mrs. Abigail Fabbershawm wrote about her life in Richmond from October 1894 to July 1928. After her death, one of her granddaughters discovered her diary and vowed to continue writing it.

> *September 14, 1912*
> The Meeting House is finished. It's really round! My parents bought a pew and my brothers have already carved their initials in it. They did it during Town Meeting Day while all the kids were running around wild.

December 15, 1914
Stamps and envelopes! Stamps are two cents each . . . Imagine! I guess it's worth the money if the letter can be hand delivered.

July 15, 1928
I met Eleanor Roosevelt! She stopped over in our town today to have tea over at Lea's Tavern. She told me how she had to wait for H.P. Brown's cows crossing at the Four Corners before she could cross. Imagine: the President's wife waiting for cows!

Abigail Fabbershawm

The class voted to borrow money from the school to help publish our booklet. There were many discussions and healthy arguments over many issues: the amount to borrow, the number of copies to print, the amount to charge for each booklet, the colors of the booklet, when and where to sell it, and how to keep track of sales. It took three class meetings and a couple of math classes to sort out all these details. They wrote articles for *The Richmond Times*, made posters, and made sales pitches for the booklet over morning announcements on our school's intercom. It was decided to give a free copy to each guest speaker and each business that had been written up. Sales as well as spirits were high. We received several letters from people in the community as well as from people from out of town (see Figure 6.3).

Evaluation of the study was an ongoing formative process. Frequent journal responses kept me informed as to what the kids were thinking and learning. The journals helped me to address problems immediately and revise my plans as necessary. I met with each student individually after completing each major part of the study. Students made a formal evaluation at the end of the study, checking off the parts they liked and disliked and listing some of the things they had learned. Perhaps I shouldn't have been as surprised as I was about their response to the question, "What will you remember most about the Richmond Four Corners study?"

How nervous and scared I used to be about talking to people I didn't know. It's nothing once you get the hang of it.

Judy

I really will remember my group project. We worked great together. We always tried to be positive and say good things to each other.

Jason

Dear Friends,

I purchased a copy of <u>A Community Study: The Richmond Four Corners</u> today from Mrs. Debbie Lawrence, mother of Gibson. While I've not yet read it all, I am impressed with its high quality.

I was particularly fond of Norma Jean's article on the Bargain Barn, since it is located directly across the street from Richmond Elementary. I spent lots of time looking out my window at it.

Keep up the good work. You make me very proud of you.

Best regards,

Barry C. Meigs
Principal

Figure 6.3. Letter from Barry Meigs, Summit Street/Thomas Fleming Elementary Schools.

I will never forget one class meeting where we fought over selling the booklet. We tried to not yell at each other and then when it was over we were all still friends.

Darren

I'm going to remember the whole thing. It was exciting (but not the editing parts). What are we going to plan next?

Jennifer

Originally, my primary goal had been to start off the year with a bang and grab everyone's attention. I also wanted to build a sense of community with my new group during our first year together. I think Jennifer captured it all when she asked, "What are we going to plan next?" She's hooked, and so am I.

Chapter 7

A View From the Park

Cristal J. Brown and Maggie Eaton

Spaulding Grade School, Barre

"Look what we've got!" This welcome refrain resounded for 6 weeks. Our students were finding information, making adult friends, and learning history. They were becoming more self-aware, and they were both mystified and challenged. Every day we heard kids exclaiming— "Look what we've got!"

The park project, as it came to be known, started simply without any particular fanfare or preteaching—just a simple beginning. An early-season storm had blanketed Barre with 2 inches of new snow, so students had worn warm jackets to class. In the school parking lot, we found another class. Were they going to the same place? How could a reading class and a science class be doing the same thing? What were we going to do?

Leading our classes to the gazebo in the middle of the park two blocks from our school, we began to wonder if we really were as insane as the kids were trying to tell us we might be:

Won't you get in trouble for bringing two classes outside?
How can we have class without our textbooks?

Who cares? It's a nice day out, and it's really neat to get out of the
room.
Look, they can't make us do any work—we didn't bring any notebooks or pencils!

The sun shone brightly on the snow in a little park downtown in a
central Vermont city known primarily for the excellence of its
stonework. (Barre is the granite center of the world!) The statue known
only to our students as "the guy with the sword" leveled his steady gaze
down Main Street, as always. Granite trucks rumbled through the
major intersection on their way to the granite sheds, where quarried
granite is finished for monuments. The streets quieted for a moment
and then groaned back to life at the change of the traffic light. The
benches somehow got wiped dry from the melting snow, and Jim
(Maggie's husband) emerged from behind the trees with his video camera. Then we began.
"What do you see?" we asked. "What could we study? What questions could we ask?" Every idea was written down on a large newsprint
pad, and students soon generated the elements of the unit.

What are these plants?
Maybe the traffic?
How about the buildings?
How long have they been here?
What are they used for?
Where can you get information? The library? City hall?
Maybe from the people who work in them.
From people who live in the senior citizens apartment?
From old newspapers?

Thirty-one eighth graders produced a lengthy list of ideas and questions. We soon exhausted time and paper. Gerard had quickly psyched
out the situation, declaring on camera, "This is certainly going to be a
great learning experience for everyone." Then we returned to school.
Ten minutes later, we heard the kids buzzing over lunch about a *new*
topic of conversation: studying our town.

NUTS AND BOLTS

Because the school schedule allowed our two classes to meet together
for only three 40-minute periods each week, we felt we needed to make

students comfortable with working on this project outside of the time and space confines of the school day. During our second class, we reviewed Jim's videotape from the first day, talking about how we felt about the project. There was still a lot of confusion because there were no specific questions to answer, no search-and-destroy questions whose answers must match those on a test key. There was also some nervous recognition and self-consciousness about seeing ourselves on videotape. We wondered further whether "important" people would have any interest in our project.

We decided to organize ourselves into ten groups of three students, neatly divided to study ten public buildings we had chosen. Every student was given the opportunity to make a first, second, and third choice of a building to study. As so many students wanted to study the fire station and city hall, where the police department is housed, special groups of four were formed to study those buildings. One of those groups later evolved into two pairs. The need for flexible groupings like these is typical of the changing needs of young adolescents.

Our class met to talk about how to ask for help with the project. As teachers, we were not looking for just library research. We had specifically chosen a project that would require our students to interact with community leaders. In class, students role-played a visit to an office, introducing each student in the group, delivering a prepared letter of introduction from their teachers, and making an appointment for a conference or interview. Gerard provided comic relief, snapping his letter open like an FBI agent to show his official identification.

We also talked about what we would like to have as products of this research. Four possible products and committees that would be responsible for them were planned: a booklet, a reenactment of an historical event, a "Monopoly"-style board game, and a videotape. Students began to understand that the project as a whole depended on everyone's contributions to the products. A sign-up sheet for product groups allowed students to make choices.

TRY, TRY AGAIN . . . AND AGAIN

Research groups were required to make a contact within the week with an adult who was knowledgeable about their building. Most were able to do so within a couple of days. On Friday morning, the science class (the reading class was unavailable) set off for the park and for various appointments with their adult contacts, sketching, or writing.

One group had not established contact with anyone concerning their building. They discussed possible ways to make a contact as we walked. In no time we found ourselves in front of the building in question, and the direct approach was suggested—in the door and up the stairs until the students found someone to talk to. Away they went. First attempt: "Oh, no! The building is under renovation. Should we go in anyway? A sign says, 'Please use rear entrance.'" Second attempt: "There are no signs inside to tell us where the office is." Third attempt: "We found an upstairs office, but no one is in there right now." A fourth try resulted in contact with someone who worked there, but everyone else was in a meeting. Then someone thought out loud, "Does the Granite Association have a telephone number?" It was surprising to note that Gerard, so cool on camera and so outgoing in class, was part of this shy team.

It would have been easier, of course, for us to go in and make the contact ourselves, explaining that our students were overcome by shyness. However, we knew that their realization of their own capabilities is an important part of growth. As the three boys struggled with their timidity, a teacher sitting in the park became a supportive base they could return to.

There were still many questions about just what we should be looking for. We brainstormed some of the things that might be interesting to know about a building: when it was built, who built it, what its original purpose was, what the architectural style was, what materials were used, what was there before it was built, and whether anything important or exciting had ever happened there. That particular activity helped more of our research groups to really dig in and get started.

Most early class periods were spent either with the two of us teachers in the gazebo in the park—conferencing, planning, and acting as home base for students out doing research—or with some students and one of us back in a classroom writing and working on research products while others were out gathering information. Students who had no specific appointments sketched architectural details, wrote poems or some other form of personal impressions, or simply noted additional things they needed to find out. One such day, Seth wrote:

The post office stands in majestic beauty,
Inside workers now do their duty
Through rain, sleet, and snow.
They move through the weather with a glow.
They will be on time . . . we know.

Damara and Erin wrote:

The Episcopal church kind of sits off by itself out of the busy streets of downtown Barre. It's a unique church. It is small and dainty, as though to welcome all people walking by.

LEARNING TO USE TIME WELL

The exhibition curator at the public library was eager to help our students, provided they made appointments. Many groups learned quickly to take full advantage of the time they had. Students who found out something interesting concerning another building readily shared it with the students in the group studying that building. Some groups made arrangements to use the school's camera, while others borrowed one or used their own. Kids photographed old pictures and materials maintained in the archives at the library.

KNOW WHAT WE FOUND OUT?

Every student and every group had unique experiences. The group studying the fire station returned one day, late as usual, wearing plastic junior fireman hats, some too small for their nearly adult-sized heads and some fitting rather well. They proudly wore them back to school, inside and up the stairs. These four—often referred to as troublemakers—were most persistent in their research, often making appointments during study halls and after school to learn more about a certain part of our fire department.

Every day the group studying the library brought back page after page of copies of old photographs, some for their own study and some to share. This group became the resident experts on where to find information on downtown Barre. One girl explained the need to wear gloves while studying old documents. They delighted in dallying amid the dust of earlier eras.

The group studying the Episcopal church excitedly spouted bits of history of the Protestant Episcopal church of the United States. As none of them attended this particular church, it was very exciting for them to learn of the history and traditions of their neighbors.

The two pairs of students studying city hall appeared with mug shots taken at the police station. One group had been fingerprinted, and several had tried out the lockup. Students were also beginning to understand some of the governmental and political structures of the city. They included the names of the current aldermen in their report.

Shortly after we began our project, we were pleased to receive a call from city hall explaining that a new issue of a local magazine featured the most exciting historical event to ever happen downtown (aside from the original city hall burning): Teddy Roosevelt had campaigned in the park in 1912 in his unsuccessful bid for a second term. Were our local important people interested in our students' projects? Most definitely! The kids were initially surprised and then excited at the realization that adults were genuinely interested in their work.

The post office group worked quietly. They had interviewed the postmaster, who was quite willing to help if they wrote out their questions. They toured the building, listened to descriptions of the building and the work that went on there, and took notes. Suddenly, these students asked us to find a safe place for a book that the postmaster had lent them. The book was the original 1911 log in which the building contractor had noted the tasks completed for the day, the number of each type of laborer and how much they were to be paid, and the weather. Entries included mention of "–30 degrees, no snow; 3 masons, 12 laborers," as well as "98 degrees, no rain; 6 carpenters." The book was not to be machine copied, so extensive handwritten notes were taken. Finding the postmaster unavailable one day, Bobby used the found time to begin a sketch of the building's facade. Encouraged by other students, he finished the drawing, which became part of the final booklet. These students delighted in telling and retelling how the first Barre postmaster would stand on the church steps, mail in the band of his tall top hat, to hand out the mail each Sunday after services were completed.

The groups studying some of the fine churches adjacent to the park soon made new friends in the pastors, historians, and older members of several congregations. Students who had never been inside all of the church buildings noted architectural details, history, traditions, and local lore. Some mentioned a new sense of comfort with church buildings other than their own church. Many pictures documented discovered treasures heretofore unnoticed.

One group studied two of the major statues downtown and the gazebo where we launched this unit. A poll taken on Main Street showed that few citizens of Barre had any idea what the statue in the center of town was all about, which afforded students a chance to become local experts.

One day while sketching and writing in the park, the group studying the statues discovered a time capsule tucked behind one of the statues. It was not very old, dating only from 1970. Just the same, it was exciting for speculation. It will be opened in the year 2000. We enjoyed wondering where *we* would be then. We were surprised to find out that the gazebo had been moved several times and that Mary Baker Eddy (founder of the Christian Science church) had moved from Barre because the band concerts at the gazebo had interrupted her meditations.

The group studying the Barre opera house learned of the splendor of bygone days, the dwindling of live theater due to television and movies, and the struggle to rebuild a fine hall for today's live performances. Kelly mentioned a lot of "sitting and thinking" while studying in and about that fine old building.

Students' excitement over their research continued long after the usual school day. Out shopping one Saturday, Maggie was set upon by Gerard's group returning from a research session at the public library. They all talked at once, mentioning old records they'd seen and their appointment with the curator for Monday's class time. What a different experience from the usual self-conscious "Hi, teacher" greetings we usually receive outside of school!

A PRODUCTION LINE

The products seemed slow in coming. We found that in light of our having only three class periods a week together, we had been overambitious. The booklet committee requested one or two written pages plus at least one photograph or drawing from each research group. Drafts were written, edited, and rewritten. A title was chosen: A View from the Park. And a typist volunteered.

Traci typed about 90% of the written material. An interesting note about Traci's typing: The special educator in our building was surprised that Traci could type such a work since she read so very little. She had been documented by the school as having written language problems, and she had struggled with all of her academics. Nonetheless, Traci worked steadily until the booklet copy was all on computer disk. We also found that Traci had submitted more than a page of *her own writing* concerning her experiences with the church she had studied. She went on to complete a fine paper for her fourth-term English project, again to the surprise of our special educator.

Another student, Margaret, became concerned about one of the kids in her group who did not seem to be doing her share of the work. It seemed that the other two group members were involved in a tiff. We talked about it with each of the girls separately, and later Margaret requested help in spelling and writing from Tanya while Traci typed. Margaret had found a way for Tanya to be needed. Although Margaret actually is a fairly good speller, she was able to draw Tanya back into the group with her conciliatory request.

The videotape committee decided on a newscast format for the portion of the tape they produced. Rehearsal time was scant, but using Maggie's classroom as our studio, we shot the needed footage. Interviews at the park were added to the footage shot at the initial session. The edited result was a 25-minute tape showing our students becoming experts and reporting on a small piece of Barre, historically and in the present day. The videotape shows students being remarkably poised and confident—being professional—as they reported on their work. Eliminating the "right answer/right conclusion" angle enabled students to *believe* that they were learning and had become experts in what they had studied.

The board game and the reenactment of a historical event did not fare as well. Although students worked at the board game concept, we found that it was really too complicated a project to be developed properly in the time we had. However, we do feel that we might have been more able to develop a game of this type had we had five class periods per week to work together and had we as teachers had daily planning time together to coordinate our ideas. Such planning time was limited to only two common periods per week. The reenactment was a project that initially drew high levels of interest, but in light of the shortage of time, we concentrated instead on the videotape and booklet.

TO TELL THE TRUTH

How did we know whether students did in fact do the work? Each student gave us a quick evaluation of his or her partner's contribution using a checkoff sheet with statements to be completed and three to five levels or choices (see Figure 7.1).

As teachers, we needed to know whether our sense of what was happening during the project matched what students were actually experiencing. An inquiry method we had previously used in coursework to assess various portions of our eighth-grade program was used. Using scrap paper cut into smallish pieces, we asked eight questions, one at a time. Students responded anonymously, and we collected all responses after each question. Then we sorted them to see what the kids had to say. Some responses were insightful, some funny, some just what we expected, and some very much unexpected. Each set of responses showed us that students had learned in ways that corresponded to our stated goals.

Evaluation of Partner's Cooperation

Partner's Name _____

This partner did:
_____ all _____ most _____ her/his share _____ very little
_____ none of the work to research and write up our building.

This partner was:
_____ very helpful _____ O.K. _____ not helpful
_____ keeping us from getting the project done.

We were able to cooperate:
_____ very well _____ most of the time _____ O.K.
_____ hardly ever _____ never

If we did another unit like this, I:
____ would ____ might ___ would not choose this partner to
work with again.

I think that I did:
_____ all_____ most _____ my share ____ some ____ none of
the work on our project.

My Name _____

Figure 7.1. Student evaluation form of partner's contribution.

To the question, "What was the best thing about this project?" the most frequent answers referred to being able to work in a group and studying on their own without constant direction. Many students commented about going outside. Being able to study things about the city that "you wouldn't usually be able to do" and meeting new people were also frequently named as best things.

As not all is positive in any endeavor, we also asked, "What was the worst thing about this project?" Many students felt that they had not had enough time to do a good job. Others felt that the worst part was ending the unit! A few students took exception to having to write. A few of them stated that making the initial contact was the worst thing. Two students felt that the teachers had supervised them too much when they were working in the classroom. Several students claimed to have a hard time finding a worst thing.

Of course, we asked students to write about one thing they had learned about the building they had studied. These responses ranged from factual—"It was the first church built in Barre"—to more sentimental—"The people there are nice" and "I learned pride." Most of them named an event and date or a person they had not known before.

As we had hoped for students to feel proud of their community, we also asked them to write about things they had learned about Barre and its environs, such as Wildersburg (previous name), or about old population and labor conditions, recognizing that things were not always as they are now. Some named things that have not changed since the settlement of Barre: "Park and Main Streets have always been there." Some pointed out that famous people have on occasion visited our town: Teddy Roosevelt and Helen Keller were both mentioned. One student stated, "It was a lot more complex than the skimpy, little town I thought it was."

A major goal of this project was to promote work within a group, so we asked for one thing each student learned about a partner. Some made a new friend. Some admitted to having revised perceptions of each other.

> She wasn't as shy as I had thought.
> He doesn't always stay on task.
> She is very impatient and demanding.
> She really is very hardworking, but likes to fool around, too.
> It's not all that bad having a girl in your group.
> Apparently everyone learned some important things about the
>   people they worked with.

We had hoped for students to grow during this experience, so we asked each student to write one thing he or she had learned about himself or herself. Most students seemed to find that they were not as shy as they had thought themselves to be, that they could get the work done if they really decided to, and that they really could work on their own. A few reported that they didn't like interviewing grown-ups and that they didn't work very hard at what they were studying because they did not find it that interesting. One student learned that she is self-conscious, and several mentioned that they need to become more patient with each other.

A standard question in this type of assessment concerns how students would change the program if they could. We asked, "What *one* thing should be changed about this project?" Many students felt that we should have much more time. There were various opinions about the groups: Some felt that two people to a group would be more effective, while others thought that larger groups of four to five students would be better. Several mentioned not wanting to be videotaped. Five students felt that there was nothing that should be changed.

A second standard question sought to identify the most vital elements of the program. We asked, "What one thing must *not* be changed?" About half of the students felt that going outside the school walls into the community and working independently were most important. One fourth of the students felt that working in groups was vital. Several thought the weather was perfect, and some thought that certain buildings or products must be part of the study. One student thought that we should not change *anything*.

This quick inquiry assured us that much of what we had hoped for was achieved: Students on many different levels learned more than facts and figures. Some learned of the resources available to them as citizens of the city. Most have shown us in a variety of ways their new respect for and interest in the community in which they live.

ALL GOOD THINGS . . .

The active working phases of the park project came to an end in mid-November. Students made posters using photographs and materials they had collected. The booklet and videotape were edited over several weeks, and a final edit for punctuation was made by the teachers. Students were given credit in the booklet as the researchers, members of the community who helped students were awarded special thanks, and we added a one-page statement about the project and the results. The final copy was pasted up into a 28-page booklet that could be printed at our school district copy center. Students collated the pages during study halls and then stapled and folded them.

In mid-January, we invited parents, friends, and all people from the community who had helped to an evening presentation of the finished videotape and booklets. The students were very proud to present their finished products at last.

We also mailed booklets to community members who were unable to attend the evening festivities and sent copies to our school administration. We believed it was important for these people to see a finished product because they had given their time and shared their expertise with us.

THE MATTER AT HEART

Was this a worthwhile experience for our students? In terms of the goals we had established, we believe that this was extremely worthwhile. Eighth graders are often caught in the limbo between childhood and adulthood. They are certainly not children anymore, but neither are they old enough to really be a part of the work force. It is so easy for them to feel alienated from their community despite their constant movement through and survival in it. Our students found that there is more to Barre than they had realized. They made some connections they would not otherwise have made. They became comfortable not just as people who live in Barre, but as citizens. They learned facts and figures, and they also learned important attitudes and developed new facets of their self-image.

We doubt whether these students will remember most of the facts and figures in the future, but they will certainly remember that the mayor took time to help them with their eighth-grade project, that they have a specific representative on the city council, that one doesn't have to be baptized in a particular church to attend services there or to seek assistance from the pastor, and that even government employees and other citizens are approachable. We know that many of our students learned that they can overcome their shyness to get a job done, that they can be persistent enough to finish a project, and that they can be respected in a community even though they are "only" schoolkids. We also know that reading, writing, questioning, explaining, and other scholarly endeavors come naturally when kids have a cause. What more could anyone hope for?

Chapter 8

Adopt a Business

Carol Smith, Linda Mann, and Warren Steadman
Shelburne Middle School, Shelburne

The Alpha team was ready. The groundwork was complete. Information had been collected and digested, and now it was time for the students to give back all that they had learned. Student-made business booths had been created—complete with advertising posters and sample products. Videotapes of interviews with business owners and on-site visits were ready for viewing. Student "businessmen" and "businesswomen" stood ready to teach what they had learned to their parents, their friends, and community people visiting them that evening. The businesspeople of the town of Shelburne were about to see themselves through children's eyes.

Twenty-six Shelburne businesses were represented at an open house at Shelburne Middle School by the 65 fourth- through eighth-grade students on the Alpha Team who had studied them. The kids had spent the previous 4 weeks learning about their town's business life by interviewing owners, digging through town records to discover business history, and spending time working as apprentices. This was the finale. Like barkers at the circus, Alpha students manned their booths and set their open house in motion.

Weeks earlier at a team meeting, the three Alpha teachers had presented their ideas for an Adopt a Business study.

What do you mean by "Adopt a Business"?
Do you mean REALLY work in a store?
How do we decide who gets to do what?
How do we pick our partners?

These and many more questions darted about our classroom at the start of this integrated study. They were wonderful, pertinent questions—just the ones we wanted our children to conceptualize and answer—questions that would lead us to discussions, research, comparisons, compromise, and eventually resolutions that would reflect choices and decisions. They were the kind of questions that allowed for individual opinion but required consensus in order to organize such a large, multifaceted team project. They were the kind of questions from which authentic learning occurs.

The idea for this interdisciplinary study of local businesses had been developed over the summer. It seemed a perfect way to involve students in their community and provide them with firsthand learning. Our goals were simple: to have students relate in-school learning to real-life application, interact with adults in their community, and work together to solve common problems. With these goals in mind, we made initial contact with 35 Shelburne business owners and obtained a tentative commitment from 30 of them to participate in our project. We sent all business owners a letter thanking them for their initial interest and restating our overall goals for our Adopt a Business study.

Integrated curriculum work is central to Alpha's philosophy, so in-depth study units were not entirely new to our students. Most recently, they had successfully completed an integrated study of Lake Champlain and another on the Civil War. An annual week-long camping trip near the end of each year was always organized as an integrated curriculum project as well.

This project was distinctive, however, because it involved the community in ways that were different for us. Community members—some of whom were parents—would be directly involved in the instruction of students. Business sites would become extensions of our classrooms. Another new dimension of this particular unit was to involve students in the actual planning and development of the study.

Jerry Greenfield from Ben and Jerry's Ice Cream Company was our kickoff speaker. He talked about the hows and whys of starting a business, explaining about developing an idea, creating a plan, and securing start-up money. He also talked about luck, hard work, and responsibility. Explanations of the pros and cons of being "my own boss" and working closely with a friend were personal as well as informative. Finally, he talked about factors affecting failure and success. And he brought ice cream to share!

A whole class discussion followed, and students talked about how to choose partners and how to most fairly pick a business to study. Their discussion was long and sometimes heated, and consensus was difficult to reach.

> Working with your friend might be fun, but it doesn't always mean that you'll get your work done.
> I can't work at all if I have to be partners with someone I don't get along with.
> Maybe we should let the teachers choose.
> Maybe we should decide what business we want to study, and pick our partners by interest.
> I work best with a friend.

Ultimately, students voted to choose their partners themselves, and they did so. With businesses willing to work with groups of two to three students at a time, partnerships were easily and quickly decided. One student chose to isolate himself from the class at this time and did not choose to be in a group. He was allowed to work on his own. In retrospect, we might have worked harder to get him into a group. At the time, however, the discipline problems likely to arise from forcing the issue were more than we wanted to deal with.

Deciding which students could adopt which business came next. Picking the fairest way to do this also came about through class discussion. The option the kids originally suggested was first come, first served; the eighth graders would pick first, and the fourth graders would pick last. Another particularly interesting option was to have a lottery drawing, thereby providing a purely random selection. Although this was seen as the most fair, students wanted to exercise more individual choice in the business they were to adopt and study.

A class vote determined our ultimate course of action. It was decided that each group would choose three businesses they were interested in, submit those to the teachers by day's end, and let the teachers sort it out. Teachers also agreed to come back to individual groups should a major problem arise with their choices.

Soon partners were chosen, and businesses were adopted. We also had commitments from the business community, and we had our overall goals set. Now we had to make the what, when, and how decisions regarding requirements and outcomes.

Discussions about what we could learn about a business and about the person who ran it consumed a lot of time at first. Sometimes the entire class met, but more often small groups worked with one teacher to list ideas. As the lists developed, ideas began to fit into categories: past history of the business, current operation of the business, and a personal profile of the owner of the business. For each of the three categories, specific questions emerged that became the basis for a business profile sheet (past and present) and an owner profile sheet.

It became clear early on that usual forms of school-based research would not provide us with all the answers. A teacher-directed discussion of alternative research methods and sources was held. Students learned that personal interviews with business owners would be the best way to learn about how businesses work. Another form of research would be necessary to provide the historical context.

We engaged the help of Pam Pomfret, the Shelburne town planner, and Colleen Haag, the town clerk. Pam spoke to the whole team at once about the history of the town, its zoning laws, and the town plan for the future. Colleen worked with smaller groups of kids digging through old town records housed in the vault at the Shelburne town hall. Learning how to trace a piece of property back to its original owner was intriguing and exciting. Kids likened the process to looking for clues to solve a mystery.

Some clues provided us with especially interesting tidbits of information. For example, the invention of the typewriter in 1828 did not immediately modernize recording methods for Shelburne. Handwritten documents were on record long after the typewriter became available. The building occupied today by the bakery was once an underground railroad station. A small office building now housing a dentist and an insurance agency was once the creamery for local dairy farmers.

Using the information acquired through this research, kids made time lines for their business properties, in some instances tracing back to the original property owner. Parents soon became involved as students pushed to discover the origins of the houses where they lived. Several children subsequently introduced their parents to Colleen and the vault. This study became quite an experience for families, too.

Interviewing was something new to most of our children. For many, talking to a relative stranger was a formidable undertaking. To prepare them, we discussed in small groups how to create a list of sample questions. Then we teachers modeled a sample interview session. Students next took turns being interviewers and interviewees. Gradually, the process became more familiar to them. The small study groups practiced their particular questions and planned who would talk, who would run the tape recorder, and who would take notes.

Telephone calls to arrange visiting dates provided students with their first personal contact with business owners. Unfamiliar as such inquiries were for some students, talking to owners and having owners be enthused about their interest helped put the children at ease and paved the way for the visits to come.

The first day of our site visits arrived. All students made brief visits to their businesses to introduce themselves, tour the facility, and set up times for future visits. Parent volunteers had been summoned to help us supervise our 65 young investigators. We needed contact people spread out in the community in case of a problem. We three teachers also spread ourselves out so as to make brief contact with each business. And it all worked beautifully! Our 65 students returned to school excited and ready to begin.

Over the next 2 weeks, students finished their work in the town offices, visited businesses, interviewed business owners, and assembled their work in the classroom. In-class time was spent transcribing taped interviews, making time lines, and creating advertising material for each business. Each of the teachers supervised one third of the business studies, conferencing regularly to ensure that groups were staying on track.

All students maintained personal journals in which they kept daily accounts of their experiences—jotting down thoughts and ideas, commenting on each stage of the study, citing both successes and difficulties, and making suggestions to teachers for future versions of Adopt a Business:

> I think we should be able to work in our business for a whole day.
> Finding the area was hard for us. There were too many shelves
>   and counters in Vermont's Own Products to do this easily.
> We had trouble making the time line. It was really hard to find all
>   the dates.
> My group couldn't decide on a poster idea. We couldn't agree on
>   the design. It didn't come out very well because we never
>   found something we all liked.

Excitement mounted as the kids' workday at their adopted businesses approached. They were scheduled to work for half the day at their businesses, and we had encouraged business owners to find appropriate ways to put them to work.

Kids at the Chittenden Bank learned how to count money as a double check for the tellers, and to their amazement they discovered an error! The Companion Hardware Store group learned how to make keys. Pet World had students feeding snakes and setting up birthing rooms for the white mice. Students scooped ice cream at Ben and Jerry's, stuffed second-notice bills at Applied Graphics, operated the cash register at Radio Shack, and re-marked sale items at the Quiltsmith. They also sorted bottles and cans at the Shelburne Supermarket, rearranged books displayed at the Village Booksmith, operated the computer at New England Travel, bagged lunches at the Shelburne Bakeshop, and made pizza at Rocky Romeo's. The list of jobs they performed is too vast for complete inclusion here.

This taste of job experience gave students concrete experience with the working world. They worked closely with their newly found adult mentors and met the public in ways that were both challenging and new to them. Some of their jobs were interesting—even exciting—and some were dull. Some students liked the repetitive jobs and felt comfortable with the busywork. Others expressed dissatisfaction. They wanted more responsibility. One student went so far as to say he wanted to be in charge of the business. Our follow-up classroom discussion centered on job training, education, unskilled labor, and skills necessary to hold various jobs. Students shared their job experiences and talked about what it takes to run a business. Although each business required different basic skills, the kids saw experience and training as essential components for moving up the career ladder.

Not all the work experiences were equally successful. One group that was unable to organize itself missed their work appointment at the Shelburne Craft School altogether. The director of this nonprofit organization became upset with them for wasting her time, and the students spent a considerable amount of their time making amends. They wrote an apology letter, set up a new work date, and offered their services to help out at the business (on their own time). Although this episode was not intended, it provided an excellent springboard for discussions about commitment and responsibility for one's actions.

The open house had been planned as the culminating event for our Adopt a Business study, and the event required students to present their businesses in ways that would demonstrate to teachers, parents, and Shelburne businesspersons just what they had learned. With less than a week to go, Patricia from POW Productions was invited to help kids figure out ways to enhance their business presentations. POW

Productions is a Shelburne business that holds workshops and seminars on how people can revitalize their business presentations by building their own self-confidence and using multisensory elements. With Pat's expertise, students learned the value of color, design, music, humor, clarity, and creativity.

Pat's presentation inspired the kids, and as soon as she finished, they immediately went to work. Presentation secrets were well guarded, and even teachers were not totally clued in prior to the final effect. Classroom space for individual business booths was assigned, and students began to set up their displays. Posters and props emerged, and tape recorders with background music were camouflaged. Costumes were also discussed. Costumes? What had been scheduled as an open house was fast turning into a major production.

Parents, school board members, administrators, and businesspeople from all over Shelburne had been invited to see Adopt a Business in action. This public presentation allowed everyone to see the pieces put together and see the unity in the study. Students were expected to demonstrate their knowledge and to apply and adapt it in lots of creative ways. They'd also have an opportunity to see and learn from each other's work—sometimes for the first time. They also made comparisons with their own work, noting different styles and presentation formats and seeing the variety of ways in which a presentation could work well. Parents got to experience their children's individual learning and to view it in relationship to the whole. Business owners got a kids' eye view of themselves and our town. And the teachers? We smiled a lot. The kids made us look good! Very good.

By 7:00 in the evening, things began to roll. Exotic bird noises from Pet World vied with a student-written rap about banking. The aroma of Rocky Romeo's pizza mixed with that of Harrington's ham as visitors were invited to taste test sample products. The Village Flower Shop was permeated with the scent of roses, and New England Travel booked reservations on a student-designed computer. The Quiltsmith offered a quilting bee, and a display of best-sellers came from the Village Bookshop. Ed-U-Care, a day-care center, offered advice about child care, and the Shelburne Supermarket discussed the pros and cons of a family-run business. Sports Style talked fashion, and Woodbury's Woodenware talked wood.

Integrated studies like Adopt a Business offer children a unique opportunity to explore, to roll up their sleeves, and to dig into something. They learned how to look at something from many angles, to question it, and to wonder about it. It was an opportunity to take apart something interesting and then put it back together in a unique and interesting way, finding new reasons and meanings for things.

For some kids, this was a first opportunity to spend meaningful time with an adult outside their family structure. For others, it was a successful experience working with a partner. For still others, it was a chance to explore the connections between education and success in later life. It was an experience that demanded fuller participation than other schoolwork. The study allowed choice and encouraged creativity, and it required discussion, compromise, cooperation, and responsibility. It allowed children to explore an immediate, accessible world beyond the classroom that they were capable of understanding.

Did this study make a difference?

Guess what I did today? I got to work the cash register! Isn't that neat? And they told me, when I'm old enough, maybe I could get a job here! Isn't that neat? This business stuff is great!

Yes, indeed—*it makes a difference!*

IV

NATURE STUDIES

Chapter 9

Weather Watch

Judith Steffens, Marlene Conru, and Paul Garrett
Founders Memorial School, Essex Town

"So, Marlene, you want us to ask children to research hurricanes, tornadoes, floods, and blizzards?" Paul paused. "That could be a real disaster!"

And so it began! Groaning as puns flew, munching our lunches as we planned, our new unit, Weather Watch, began to take shape. Our three-person team was to have many such lunchtime meetings. Initially we brainstormed aloud, searching for ideas that would capture the interest of the 75 fifth graders we teach and that would capitalize on our individual strengths and passions as teachers. Fortunately, we were comfortable working together; we had been team teaching for 4 years. Generally, Paul was responsible for teaching math and science; Marlene also taught math, in addition to reading and social studies; and Judy concentrated on social studies and language arts. However, it was clear that if this unit were to be truly integrated, we'd each need to extend ourselves to do a little bit of everything.

One of our first decisions was that we would offer three different mini-units from which the children could choose. Because Marlene loved teaching literature, the primary focus of her mini-unit, Conru's

Disaster, would be researching and reading about weather disasters. Students who selected Paul's mini-unit, Masters of Meteorology, would create their own weather instruments in a science lab setting. Judy's mini-unit, a travel bureau later dubbed by the students who selected it as Gone With the Wind Travel, would involve kids in lots of writing and speaking activities. Together, we created activities that would incorporate additional content areas into our units, relying heavily on each other for suggestions about subjects we didn't ordinarily teach. Each night, we'd individually add to the plan for our separate mini-units and then get together the next day for each other's critiques and suggestions. As our mini-units became more defined, we invited the music and art teachers, the learning center coordinator, and the science coordinator to join our team meetings.

We decided to establish some common academic expectations for all three mini-units, whatever their focus. Each student, for example, would be asked to read at least two weather-related literature books and to share those books with the class. Each was also asked to write an original weather myth to link up with a study of mythology we'd begin once Weather Watch had been completed. We then drew up a master list of the skills that we could teach while using weather as a focus. These skills were drawn from the extensive curricula for which we're accountable in our district, and they ranged from differentiating between cause and effect to reading graphs and charts. We're always astonished at how easily the skills that seem formidable in the abstraction of a list can actually be incorporated through a unit such as this. This list of more than 40 skills was also a great help during parent conferences, particularly with parents who were apprehensive that our integrated approach might neglect the basics. The list was further helpful as a record-keeping tool, and we found that our list grew as the children's enthusiasm led us into areas different from those we'd envisioned earlier when planning our mini-units.

With a much clearer vision of Weather Watch and the mini-units of which it would consist, we began using our lunchtime planning sessions to deal with the logistical problems created in part by the number of students for whom we were responsible and the limitations of a schoolwide master schedule. Some of the most urgent questions and our subsequent strategies follow.

What preteaching would need to be done for students in all three mini-units?
Paul spent 1 week with all three groups reviewing basic weather information.

Where could we get the materials we'd need for an integrated study that would involve 73 students?
Our learning center coordinator was very helpful, and a Chapter II grant from the state allowed us to purchase what we didn't own, including an Apple computer, software, and a multitude of paperbacks.

When would we meet and for how long?
We set aside from 1 to 2 hours a day for 4 weeks.

How could we gain the necessary knowledge to teach well?
Several workshops with a local forecaster gave us a rudimentary background that Paul expanded on.

This preliminary planning later proved to be invaluable. In integrated units we had taught previously, we had discovered that once the students become involved, the units take off—often rapidly and in different directions from what we'd envisioned. This time, our preliminary planning meant that we were organized enough so that flexibility was possible. We knew what materials were available, we could direct students to resources in and out of school, and we were confident that important skills were being learned—wherever students' interests led them. We felt comfortably accountable throughout the unit; we knew what we were teaching and what remained to be explored. We were also able to use our time with students to teach and facilitate. We seemed to avoid the frenetic scrambling for materials and ideas and the continual seat-of-the-pants decision making that can occur if a unit hasn't been adequately preplanned. We were busy and excited—but on the inside, we were basically calm!

Finally, Weather Watch began. We gathered all the students together for a Weather Watch pep rally, in which we explained our ideas and showed examples of the kinds of things students might be doing. Students were asked to make first and second choices among the sections and to give reasons for their decisions. As might be expected with children this age, their responses revealed a lot about themselves. Erica, for example, picked Conru's section with an earnest expression on her face, explaining that she "chose disasters because whenever I would be talking to a friend and someone would mention a tornado or a hurricane, I would always stop what I was doing and listen!" Sara picked travel because "It's time people learn the truth about Texas! It's an awesome place!" Chris chose meteorology because:"I'd much rather create and build than write." And there was, of course, the teacher pleaser who wrote, "I have a good feeling about this because in my mind it seems fun, exciting, educational, and neat!" Almost all the responses were exclamations showing enthusiasm and excitement. The children liked having a choice, and they were anxious to share their feelings about their choices with us and their peers. To sustain their enthusiasm, we sent home colorful notices telling parents about our work and inviting them to discuss the study with their children.

From that point on, our momentum came primarily from the students. The first day of the travel section, Brian arrived red faced and chuckling, wearing a ten-gallon cowboy hat that his parents had brought back from Wyoming. He was clearly an inspiration to others, who subsequently appeared in Levi's and cowboy boots. Within a few days, students were researching their states, contacting local travel agencies to ask for suggestions. They also began tracking the weather in their states on a wall-sized map we had made, collecting data that would later be used in a variety of graphs and charts. Kids traveled back and forth between the classroom and the learning center, and—as their research progressed—to the computer lab, where they inputted information about their states into a data base program, the *Bank Street Filer*. A very patient parent volunteer, Barbara Newman, helped the children set up the fields and format for their research; she remained astonishingly calm in the midst of chaos—even when a student accidentally bent the first data disk before a backup copy had been made! Fellow students who had just spent hours laboriously typing in information were not so calm, however, and a battle was barely avoided!

Students in the disaster group began reading a variety of titles, including *Avalanche, Call It Courage, The Night of the Twister,* and *Earthquake.* We were all delighted by their involvement in the books they read. As they enthused about a book, other children—even the more reluctant readers—were drawn in. In fact, books like *The Night of the Twister* became so popular that students worked out their own schedule for sharing them. Cries of "Keep reading . . . I'm waiting for that book!" were commonplace. This enthusiasm carried over to their homes as well, and we discovered that many of the parents were reading books their children had chosen for the unit. Little Carmen, for example, her earnest eyes bleary from lack of sleep (she'd been reading *Avalanche),* reported that she "cheered when the book ended and Chris was rescued. I was SO excited! Now my mom is reading the book to see why I liked it so much."

The students also became quite caught up in their research and showed real ownership of it. One group, known affectionately as the Floods, floated about the room imparting bits and pieces of knowledge they'd learned. Their action prompted the Tornadoes to reply, "Oh yeah? Well, look at this—six tornadoes in 1 hour. It's incredible!" We were surprised at how possessive students became about their research ("Wait a minute—you can't do that. *I'm* studying tornadoes!"). This enthusiasm replaced the more familiar moans and groans that kids made about doing the necessary research. Kids were eager to get to the learning center, and they required very little supervision or prompting.

A visit from Mark Brean, a public radio weather forecaster from the St. Johnsbury Museum, heightened their interest further. His resonant voice seemed to fascinate the students, and they were really caught up in his stories of weather phenomena. The students themselves were surprised by the extent of their own interest. As Matt put it: "If anyone had told me two weeks ago that I'd be real interested in hearing about a bunch of clouds, I'd have thought they were crazy!" One group of students asked Mr. Brean about weather folklore and then spent days trying to figure out whether there was any truth in the folklore that cows lying down meant rain or that a red sky at dawn signaled an approaching storm.

Masters of Meteorology students were constantly on the move. They took weather readings using the weather station in the school lobby, prepared weather maps based on data from local weather stations, made weather predictions, and finally verified the accuracy of their forecasts. Michael wrote:

> The thing that I liked most in Weather Watch was forecasting the weather. It made me feel good when my forecasts were correct!

Students researched weather phenomena and worked on individual projects that included weather instruments, cloud photos, and three-dimensional representations of weather events. A visit to television station WCAX to hear Stewart Hall, a local weather forecaster, and a trip to the St. Johnsbury weather station and planetarium were highlights for this group. Chris summed it up: "Saint J. was intense. I couldn't believe I was there!"

Every Friday, we gathered all three groups of children together in Paul's room, and reporters from each mini-unit shared what their group was doing. There was always a lot to talk about, but initially the students were intimidated by having to make presentations before a large audience of their classmates. They either stood beet red and silent or read in a monotone what they'd prepared. We were surprised because many of them were the same children who had been driving us crazy in class because they felt such an immediacy about what they were learning that they were constantly interrupting others. Mike, for example, who would rather talk than do research, was continually interrupting with comments preceded by, "I know you guys are busy, Mrs. Steffens, but you just have to hear this!"

We had originally intended to videotape these sharing sessions, but the kids' self-consciousness led us to abandon that idea. They were also worried that they might not give an accurate picture of what was happening in class. Ellen wrote:

> I hated being secretary and reporter because if I wrote, I couldn't listen. And when I'd ask someone if something was right, they'd say, "Didn't you listen?"

The problem was solved by having several children work together to organize and present what had happened each week. By the time we had our final sharing session, almost everyone was comfortable in front of the large group because they knew their audience was genuinely interested in what they had to say. These general sessions were also used to show some videos and films we'd obtained. They represented quite a mix, from Bell Laboratories' *Unchained Goddess* to *The Wizard of Oz*, enthusiastically requested by the Tornadoes, who had vivid memories of Dorothy heading for the storm cellar!

Our general sessions seemed to help students keep in touch with what was happening in all three mini-units. Students seemed very proud of what their group had done. You could always pick out the most proud ones when their group was presenting: They'd be sitting forward, their faces mirroring their reactions. They also provided a wonderful opportunity for each student to feel like a part of a larger team.

What was less successful was our sustained contact with parents and community. We had planned to send home a weekly newspaper to keep parents informed of what we were doing, although we knew from the children's comments that parents were already very involved. This was fortunate, as the intended weekly report fell by the boards when we got increasingly busy working with students. We did manage to submit an article for the *School News*, a districtwide newsletter. We also recognized the need for more regular communication with parents in future units. Next year, we'll have student editors for a weekly newsletter filled with student-generated information. For this initial version of Weather Watch, however, our planned parent evening would have to suffice.

By the end of week 3, we were heading toward our Weather Watch finale. With the help of the music teacher, students prepared "You Are My Sunshine" and "Raindrops Keep Falling on My Head" to add a light touch to our presentation. The art teacher worked with us on murals and scrolls featuring illustrated weather poetry. Meanwhile, the travel group set up booths decorated with student-created posters, brochures, graphs, charts, weather information, and souvenirs they'd scavenged from friends and neighbors who had traveled in their selected states and postcards received from imaginary friends traveling there (for example, "Dear Freddy, I'm at Mount Rushmore and it's incredible! Lincoln's nose is 20 feet long. . . . That should make Jennifer feel better. . . .").

They also worked hard in preparing promotional talks and videos about the state they'd researched. Several students were surprised to find that they weren't impressed by the state they'd researched, and they were concerned that promoting it wasn't right. Somehow they were firm believers that in a report, you must have positive things to say if you're going to say anything at all. Once they were convinced that they were free to express their own opinions, they relaxed and simply wrote the report speaking candidly and eliminating the qualifiers they'd originally included. Sara, for example, began her report with:

> Forget going to Louisiana. It rains all the time. I've been following it
> for 11 days and it hasn't been sunny yet! Even Vermont is sunnier!

A chorus of "Oh mys" rang out from the class as she spoke. Other students became so enamored of the area they'd researched that they'd convinced their parents to include it in their summer plans, promising that they'd come back "with all kinds of information for next year's class!"

The disaster group filled the hallways at eye level with colorful storystrips—cartoonlike versions of books they'd read and enjoyed. These storystrips were responsible for some fairly significant traffic jams, as other students paused on their way to class to enjoy them. Their exhibit area was also filled with book posters and warning signs telling the unsuspecting what to do in case of a weather disaster. The artwork was very dramatic! One poster labeled "This could happen to you!" showed a picture of a tornado with a pair of sneaker-clad feet sticking out of the funnel. Their research reports were typed and bound, ready for viewing. In addition to some very accurate, specific information about their disasters, students included safety precautions couched in the language of a child. One child, impressed by the dangers of an airtight home exploding during a tornado, wrote:

> Don't forget to open the windows during a tornado. Otherwise, you'll
> have a *real mess!*

Her warning was accompanied by a picture showing the family dog traveling feet first out the window!

The Masters of Meterology had worked frantically to complete their projects. They hovered about anxiously once their hall display was finished. Their research reports were used as the basis for informational talks entitled Meet the Expert, which they presented to students in their homeroom. Each child courageously presented a lecture and demonstration on his or her research topic. It was not an easy task because the audience consisted of 25 students, each of whom saw himself or herself as the real expert!

The 4 weeks we'd allowed for Weather Watch went by all too quickly. Parents joined us for an evening of presentations, song, and displays. They later munched on what had for the occasion been dubbed sunshine brownies and raindrop cookies, which the students had baked with the help of cafeteria personnel. Many parents spent an hour or more browsing through the exhibits and asking questions of student guides. Students and teachers alike were surprised at the amount of information we'd gathered in such a short time and at how knowledgeable we had become about the weather. A common refrain was, "I can't believe we did all this."

The following day, all 75 students met for a final sharing. The kids offered impressions of various parts of the unit—some verbally and others in writing. Students had obviously learned a great deal. One child reported:

> Before Weather Watch, I never really paid much attention to the
> weather, but now I feel good knowing why and how certain weather
> changes occur. The only problem is that my sister is getting tired of
> hearing what kind of clouds are out each day.

Another child wrote:

> I learned a lot from Weather Watch. Some of the things were how to
> be neat, how to make a report, how to take notes, and how to find
> books that fit my topic and *me!*

We learned, too. It's impossible to overestimate the enthusiasm for learning that units such as Weather Watch can generate among students and teachers. Feedback from student journals urged us to "keep doing these fun units," "think about just doing units like this and forget the boring stuff," and "start a new Weather Watch next week." Students liked the variety of activities and the freedom of choice they were given. As Ben put it:

> I liked the projects because we could do whatever we wanted and no one would be on our backs telling us that we had to hurry up and get done or we are doing it all wrong.

They also liked the amount of movement and physical activity that was involved. Jeremy wrote:

> The best thing about this was that I didn't have to stay in my seat and do dittoes. We got to go down to the weather station and to the learning center and to go outside and do LOTS of other stuff!

Many others echoed Jeremy's feelings, and we made a mental note to remind ourselves to include this kind of movement in whatever units or lessons we teach in the future.

The Weather Watch unit we'd just completed had gone far beyond the parameters we'd originally envisioned when we were first planning the unit. The children's energy, enthusiasm, and curiosity had led us into some unanticipated investigations such as weather folklore and journalism, which benefited all of us. We learned a great deal as teachers, too—both about the weather and about working with our students. We know that the success of Weather Watch depended in large part on our encouragement of student choices and initiative and on the hands-on, active ways of learning that we built into the unit. To be sure, however, there are things we'll do differently next year. The parent newsletter is just one example.

The extensive planning we did was just the beginning. No amount of preplanning can ever sufficiently anticipate the directions a unit will take when it is driven by the seemingly limitless curiosity of 10- and 11-year-old children. Nor would you want it to. Much of the excitement that builds during an integrated study occurs when you and the children learn and explore new territory together. All of us, students and teachers alike, expended an incredible amount of emotional and intellectual energy throughout the 4 weeks we worked on Weather Watch. Although we were tired, it was worth it! There's no question that we'll do the unit again and that we'll continue to add new integrated units each year. We're convinced that whatever the setting, this kind of teaching is a possible dream. The work added enthusiasm and energy to our teaching, and we've been revitalized as a result.

Chapter 10

Go With the Flow

Ken Bergstrom
Duxbury Elementary School, Duxbury

Directly behind the Duxbury Elementary School, the Winooski River flows on its way through Central Vermont to Lake Champlain. Sometimes in the spring, it floods the playground. It has swallowed up a misguided soccer ball more than once. Kids often stand at the fence atop its bank and stare, yell, or throw stones and snowballs into the current. Stories of after-school adventures at the river's edge abound.

It had been obvious to me for some time that the river constituted an exceptionally rich topic for my students to investigate. In my most recent years of teaching, I'd learned that my fifth and sixth graders needed something more in their school lives than the traditional elementary school curriculum. The K–6 scope of a 100-student country school does not always meet students' emerging early adolescent needs for a more dynamic, intense, and engaging learning experience. The river would become the focus of our fall study.

PACED THE SAME

I began the year with 18 fifth and sixth graders. About half had spent the previous year with me, so there was already a bond of classroom

120

trust. I had students willing to help me devise a productive and interesting school year. Veteran students quickly oriented the fifth graders to my style and expectations. Building on a tradition of cooperative learning, this class began to come together sooner than most other groups I'd taught.

And to my surprise, the class and I seemed to be paced the same. I have experienced many groups that needed to be held back and a few that needed to be pushed. But I had never had the pleasant experience of a class that had such a similar approach to learning as I had. Maybe this correspondence was a reflection of my development as a teacher: I have gone beyond simply being a developmentalist to tuning into the idiosyncratic needs of each particular class. These students and I soon developed a deep understanding and respect. Many days, it was like working with a group of adult colleagues. We exchanged compliments and criticisms to redirect or improve the course of the river study. Intuitively, I felt that beginning the school year with an exciting topic and a responsive class would produce wonderful results.

I sent a letter home to parents that explained my goals and presented a general outline for our river unit. I promised to keep parents informed of our progress and invited their questions and participation. The kids' excitement about our study overflowed to home, and I received positive comments from a few parents about their kids' interest in school. Parents looked forward to an open house to learn more about the project.

ON THE ISLAND

The summer had provided me with time and impetus to develop a plan for a river study. Discussions with teaching friends convinced me to involve students in the planning, especially concerning particulars such as what they wanted to learn and which activities would help them to do so. Their cooperation would increase proportionally with their involvement in designing the unit.

On the 3rd day of school, I grabbed a 12-foot-long 2 x 10 plank and led my class past the school fence across a neighbor's property and down the river bank. As the fall water level was low, the plank spanned the flow from the bank to the edge of a low-water island. We carefully crossed the plank one at a time and circled this gravel island in the middle of the Winooski. "Make a list of all the things that come to mind when you think of the river." After 15 minutes of writing on lapboards, the real-life appeal of the river environment distracted students from their lists. Natural curiosity took over: blue heron tracks, an animal hole, gull prints, a dead crayfish, algae, and flat stones to skip. I insisted that students add all these discoveries to their lists as we shared them.

Within a few days, the island disappeared under the rising river, so we were unable to go there again. However, that was the first of many almost daily visits to the river.

The brainstormed lists provided a lesson in concept mapping. On the blackboard, we practiced concept mapping. I then asked each individual to prepare a concept map from our brainstormed list of river stuff. The following day, we shared these individual mind maps in small cooperative learning groups. The task was to integrate all ideas and develop a composite mind map that could delineate directions for the study.

From these concept maps evolved several distinct aspects of the river:

River as a physical thing
River as a natural resource
River as an ecosystem
River as power and energy
River as recreation
River as history
River as a metaphor

The students had realized all of the concepts except the last two. As I led them to a discussion of the river's past, they began to understand that the river had been there for centuries. They knew bits of its history through stories of Abenaki Indian sites and their grandparents' accounts of the flood of 1927. But it was difficult for them to think abstractly about the symbolism and poetry of the Winooski. I would help them make that connection.

I subsequently presented the seven lists of activities I had developed during the summer as well as my own mind map. The kids were very excited to recognize the congruence of our thoughts. One comment expressed the level of student involvement:

No teacher ever asked me what I wanted to learn about before. I thought it was very fun when we were down at the river because it was probably the only time I ever really noticed the real beauty of it. I liked the island, but I didn't like the way it was polluted.

B. A.

I didn't really like doing mind maps alone. Group mind map was fun. I learned a lot of group skills that day.

N. A.

I liked the way we planned things together.

B. T.

We began keeping personal daily journals to document and evaluate each day's activity. Early on in the unit, some of the activities ran long, so journaling had to be done the following day. Time to digest our experiences helped improve the quality of kids' comments. Ten minutes of journal time followed by selective sharing became the routine for daily discussion of our progress. "What could we have done to improve the activity? What did we learn?" These questions and class discussions became the focus for my own journal. My writing also evolved as a valuable barometer of the further development of our study.

POETRY SPIN-OFF

As the kids were not yet aware of the metaphorical potential of the river, I introduced a poetry lesson early in the study. They had little background in writing poetry. After a general discussion about poetry form, we focused on free verse and phrases and words that could create sensory images. Each student produced a draft of a river poem. I reviewed the drafts and found a central theme that I thought would make sense to young adolescents. To the children, the river seemed to possess different moods: It was angry when it flooded, it was busy when it powered a turbine, it was peaceful when it pooled, and it was happy when it cascaded. We would personify the river.

I chose the six most mentioned moods: peaceful, friendly, busy, angry, beautiful, and full of wonder, and then I asked students to rewrite how the river might express each one. Six groups formed to combine classmates' ideas into six verses. I had expected too much. Because of their relative inexperience with poetry, groups became frustrated. I intervened and accepted the task of organizing their ideas into a final draft.

It pleased the kids to identify their individual contributions to the class poem, and I enjoyed the chance to add a few touches of my own. We were all very proud of our poem, "I Am the River," so we developed a bulletin board display for the school. Our personal graphic representations of river life, from kayakers and canoers to bobcats and algae-covered pools, decorated and accented our river poem. We now understood the river personified: It had moods like us. It symbolized life.

I Am the River

I am the river . . . peaceful . . .
running so calmly, quietly,
gently glistening and sparkling,
down my channel, on a hot day, flowing,
reflecting the rays of the sun . . .
small ripples interrupting my velvet-smooth glide.
Come, wait, enjoy this cool, quiet plac . . .
sitting, thinking, reading, working, playing.
I am the peaceful river.

I am the river . . . friendly . . .
glistening with a smile as I pass shining happy
in the sun. Inviting you, beseeching you,
to drink, to jump right in, to play, to swim.
Shooing fish toward your pole, pushing against
your paddles, coaxing you along down my entire length,
I am the friendly river.

I am the river . . . busy . . .
forcing my current on the banks, eating into the
channel, moving the rocks, dirt, silt, whirling
rapidly around stones, changing moods, pushing rafts,
canoes, and boats, turning the wheel of the mill to make
flour,
surging through power plants' electricity,
struggling against pollution, after the rains,
cleaning myself of germs, trash, sewage.
Never-ending, always chasing what's around the
next bend . . .
I am the busy river.

I am the river . . . angry . . .
my fierce temper rising after the heavy rain . . .
perhaps in revenge for poor treatment.
Crushing rocks, eroding soft muddy earth,
ripping trees and animals from the foaming banks,
dragging
them down my churning, winding path, flooding the
island,
bursting my boundaries, confusing fish with the mixing
currents,
plunging the muddy raft into the rocks, popping it!
Slapping canoes full of people into rocks, crashing them!
Rushing madly to the lake, hesitating at nothing . . .
I am the angry river.

I am the river . . .   beautiful . . .
clean currents, full of color, attracting pretty
fish, lovely wildlife, whispering waves, brushing
the flowers on the bank, soft ripples, splashing
the rocks on the sandbar, bursting into a sparkling
waterfal . . .   cascading to the bright blue pool,
sending up a lacelike rainbow in the mist.
As the last rays of the sun give me a golden,
glistening glow, magically . . .
I am the beautiful river.

I am the river . . .   full of wonder . . .
Where is my source, my beginning?
Where does my journey take me? each turn—each new
place?
Where will I end? do I ever end? am I ever the same?
What of my moods: waves, ripples, floods, trickles,
waterfalls?
And those who use me: plants, fish, birds, reptiles,
amphibians, mammals, the people, the children,
do they wonder about me? Am I the source of life?
I am the energetic water, mysterious,
I am the wonderful river.

FIGURING OUT THE GRAPH MAP

The combination of kids' involvement in planning combined with their
anticipation of activities to come helped keep us focused through a
number of traditional, not-so-exciting classroom activities. I wanted
the kids to learn the parts of a river and how it operates before we
examined the course of the Winooski. An imaginary river diagram
helped us to label parts and understand a river's evolution. Then a
worksheet on Vermont rivers led us to create a large wall map of the
Winooski River watershed area.

Two boys volunteered to stay late one afternoon to trace the outline
of the map. On the way home, one of the boys commented on how he
couldn't wait to begin the river unit. When I informed him we were
well over a week into our study, he exclaimed, "Oh, yeah, I guess we
are." Our continuous planning had become part of the project. Distinctions between preparation and learning had blurred.

As we located and labeled the tributaries and sites along the
Winooski, kids recognized places they had visited. There were many
questions and comments:

My uncle took me fishing at that dam.
Why does it start at Peacham Pond?
How can a river flow north?
Can we go to the mouth of the river?

I distributed copies of an elevation map of the Winooski watershed. It was very difficult to read and understand the cross-section drawing. One student explained it as a side view; another called it a graph map. As we traced the river's journey from its source at Peacham Pond at 1,350 feet above sea level to Lake Champlain at 93 feet above sea level and watched the tributaries join the flow, understanding of the broad reach of our river began to emerge.

> I liked how we got to know the tributaries and the source of the Winooski River, but it was hard to learn how to use the graph map.
>   *T. C.*

> I liked the map and the things we did with it. I also thought that the river from the side view was neat. I would like you to make a larger map of the Winooski watershed and have us name the brooks and rivers. I thought learning that way was hard to an extent.
>   *B. T.*

ACCESS TO THE RIVER

With the river so close to our classroom, ecological investigations were natural activities. After a discussion of animals that visit the river and preferred foods that might attract them, small groups established track pits by loosening and smoothing the sand on the river bank and baiting each area. The following day, nearly every group discovered some animal prints to cast in plaster and to identify. We also used string to outline a grid of mini-areas about a foot square on the shoreline. We recorded water temperatures, collected plant and soil specimens, and brought water samples inside to examine with microscopes. In retrospect, I didn't allow enough time for students to examine thoroughly these areas of individual interest. They also needed direct instruction in and practice with the use of microscopes. Thus, some groups were disappointed in their microscopic examinations; others were surprised by the creatures they discovered.

> I liked doing the mini-area because you learned about the river more by studying an area that is small. I also liked the microscopic view because it's neat to see what is in the river that we can't see.
>   *R. F.*

I liked the track pits because they gave us an idea of what visits the river and what they eat. I really liked the microscopic view because I like to work with a microscope and I like how you can see what is in the river water.

B. T.

WHERE DOES IT END?

From early in our investigation, students wanted to know where the river ended. I knew that a trip to its delta was essential to our study. I like to preview all my field trips ahead of time to avoid confusion, wasted time, and surprises, so one misty Sunday afternoon I visited the mouth of the Winooski River at Lake Champlain between Burlington and Colchester, Vermont. The Winooski Valley park district had created a natural area that begged for further study.

In response to my request, the Department of Environmental Studies in the School of Natural Resources at the University of Vermont sent us three self-guided tours developed by college students for that delta marsh area. The day before our trip, we spent the afternoon studying and discussing the brochures about the delta marsh. The kids noticed that each tour guide had chosen to emphasize a different aspect of the same area: the geological nature of the site, the vegetation of the spot, and the variety of wildlife found there. It was exciting to hear my students make assumptions about the writers of these self-guided tour descriptions:

This one seems to know a lot about poisonous plants.
This person seems mostly interested in the shape of the land and the water.
This person talks about why so many animals live there.

It was a wild, windy, late September day when we bused to the mouth of the river. We parked upstream and followed the river to a thickly weeded marsh where we tromped and squished out to the lake. The kids remarked about the old bed of the railroad, about many of the plants they recalled from our reading, about the many different waterfowl, and about the shape of the delta.

Ever since the first day on the island, my class had shown concern for the preservation of the river's natural beauty. One quiet boy had picked up an old rusty headlight and deposited it in the school dumpster. On each succeeding visit, more river debris was collected and trashed appropriately. So, on our way back through the delta marsh, I surprised the kids with garbage bags and a team competition cleanup.

Not one complaint! The trash they collected nearly burst the bags. I was so proud. Keeping our wild places clean seems so much more important to them than it was to my generation at that age.

On our way back to school, we stopped and wandered around the restored Ethan Allen homestead. We imagined ourselves among the first white settlers paddling up the Winooski River. What an exciting day!

Today I really enjoyed because I was outside all day and I was with all of my friends. We went through a marsh and walked alongside Lake Champlain. I enjoyed the nature walk but I didn't like it when the wind blew sand into our faces. I also liked the contest where we had to see which group could pick up the most trash.

J. B.

I liked it when we went through the marsh because the cattails were so tall I couldn't see. It was strange the way the lake shoved the river the opposite way to form the spit. I liked it when we walked across the sand.

J. I.

I learned about the different plants like touch-me-not and all the nettles. I also like the marsh because Rachel, Liz, and I played alligator.

J. K.

OLDSTERS AND YOUNGSTERS HAVE MUCH TO SHARE

The secretary of the Waterbury Historical Society visited us and shared a pictorial lecture about the Winooski's devastating flood of 1927. She then led us on a walkabout through the villages of Waterbury and Duxbury Corner, which helped bring to life the actual damage caused by that flood. Watermarks still visible on the second floor of brick buildings provoked our wonder. We learned of the Cutting family, who were washed to their death while trying to raft to safety. We heard of the repair effort that brought help from many volunteers all over the Northeast.

Through the Historical Society, groups of students contacted six survivors of the flood who were willing to be interviewed. Students created interview questions, practiced interviewing techniques with each other, telephoned to schedule afternoon appointments, and subsequently met with the flood veterans. Copies of interview tapes were given to the survivors, and original tapes were donated to the Historical Society.

It was the 60th anniversary of that great flood. Our new elderly friends shared their vivid memories enthusiastically. We learned how the young banker had taken wet money home to dry in the oven. Another group discovered how two railroad workers were stranded in the depot water tower for 3 days. Another group found out about the 45 people who spent the night on the second floor of an old home and who were the last to hear from the doomed Cutting family. In addition to the wonderful anecdotes that were shared, the children and the old-sters thoroughly enjoyed each other's company. I was impressed with the maturity with which my kids handled themselves. Without exception, students came away bubbling with exciting stories from flood veterans. What a marvelous way to help kids develop a sense of history!

> I liked doing the interview because it was fun and I learned a lot. Francis Spaulding had a lot to say like when the flood came a lot of people said, "Heck, we won't have a flood." But when it did come, they weren't ready at all. But sixty years later, we will be ready for it first in case it does come again.
>
> K. M.

> I liked doing the interview and learning about other interviews because it was fun learning about the different opinions of people who were my age at the time of the flood. I also liked the stories that some people told.
>
> J. K.

> The things I learned from the flood survivors were that the times were tough but people seemed to pull together a lot more. Today is the sixtieth anniversary.
>
> S. M.

HARNESSING THE RIVER'S POWER

Our study of the 1927 flood led us to find out about the flood control projects of the Winooski River Valley. The Waterbury Dam on the Little River and the DeForge Hydro Plant at Bolton Falls were nearby and convenient to study.

Being at the dams brought the facts, figures, and diagrams to life. The kids learned about the Civilian Conservation Corps in the early 1930s and were awed by the amount of work it took to build a dam. Tours with the operators helped students to understand the operation of power plants. We were especially thrilled at the force of the water when a plant manager opened one of the needle valves at the end of a spare penstock.

> Today I learned that over 2,275,000 cubic yards of material were used to make the dam. I also found that the water could be shut off in the tunnel by lowering a 26-ton gate. The thing that I will be able to remember the most is when they turned on the valve.
>
> *J. M.*

A series of worksheets about dams, mills, and hydroelectricity provided background and context for these field trips. On one of our trips, a walk out to a small sandbar in the river for a short discussion turned up more heron and raccoon tracks reminiscent of those we'd found earlier back at school. Sitting on that sandbar watching the kids and the waterfall dance in the autumn sunshine, I reflected on the value of field trips—firsthand learning outside of school buildings. Learning about dams and hydropower made sense when we could see and hear it happening. Then we climbed to a cliff overlooking the falls—an old Abenaki Indian site—to eat our bag lunches.

> I really enjoyed the Bolton Dam because when you watch the waterfall it looks so peaceful and beautiful. The cascade is a gorgeous site. I learned that you can either run the systems here or in Burlington by computer. The Bolton Dam is what you call a gravity dam.
>
> *J. B.*

Later, we followed the canoe portage trail around the dam. There was also extra time for exploring caves and playing games, some essentials of childhood.

IT MUST BE BIODEGRADABLE

To simply enjoy the river's recreational aspect, I planned a miniature raft race. We agreed on rules for raft dimensions, no hands-on help from adults, and most important, the use of all natural materials so we wouldn't pollute. We knew we would probably not be able to retrieve our rafts, so "biodegradable" became our watchword. We spent a couple of afternoons designing, building, and redesigning our rafts. Many kids spent hours at home; few spent no extra time. On the morning of the race, we named our ingenious crafts and disqualified two boats, one for its size and another for obvious adult help. We agreed to let them run anyway behind the rest of us.

The race did not go at all as I had imagined. The starting gate I had spent hours building failed miserably, so each of us tossed our raft into the water. Only about half the rafts were ever accounted for; even fewer finished the 1/3-mile course. Despite these disappointments, the lessons learned were valuable. When I asked how we could explain to adults what we had learned from this activity, the list grew faster than expected: to use tools, to plan a design, to measure, to try new ideas, to understand buoyancy, to watch river currents, to follow the rules, and to be a good sport.

I learned that sometimes putting your best effort into things doesn't always mean it's better. I tried to find my boat but I didn't succeed. I really liked my boat and I wish I had got it back. I planned my whole night on my boat. I guess you could say I was disappointed because my boat had failed me.

J. S.

I learned that the longer you take doesn't mean it's better. That the way the water flows affects the speed of the rafts. That the building took a long time but it was worth it. That it is very important that what you make is biodegradable because you usually can't catch the raft.

R. F.

I learned how to use tools more freely than before, the way you are supposed to hold a jackknife. But most of all, I had fun even if I didn't come in any place. I also learned that bragging about your boat doesn't get you first place.

E. B.

SLUDGE . . . YUK!

At the junction of the Dog River and the Winooski River lies the Montpelier Water Pollution Control Facility—the state of the art in Vermont. We received a courteous and thorough tour of the waste-water treatment plant. The kids had excellent questions, especially about how really clean the water could get before being discharged into the river:

How does the waste get here?
How long do the solids stay in the tank?
How much methane does it take to heat the plant?
How can you live with the smell?
Is this as clean as you can get the water?
What happens if it overflows?

Students were very interested in the methane digesters, the sludge beds, and "Big Foot," the flotation-tired sludge-fertilizing truck used at neighboring farms. Although the smell was sometimes overwhelming, the kids' genuine concern for the quality of water in the river kept their questions on track.

> After watching this operation, I don't think I'll ever drink city water again. I'm not trying to give these guys a bad name, actually it's pretty amazing how they work their machines. I had a good time aside from the smell.
>
> *N. A.*

> I learned that in the second tank the solids floated. I learned that their truck has flotation tires. They never get used to the smell. The sludge is used for fertilizer.
>
> *J. M.*

> I learned the process to get the water clean. I learned what a sludge bed was. I learned that methane was used to heat the plant.
>
> *J. I.*

I'M INCLINED TO GO

The culminating activity of our Winooski River study was to be a 9-mile canoe adventure from Montpelier downstream to Duxbury. I zipped off a letter to Clearwater Sports, local outfitters and river guides, to ask if they could help us end the river study. I also wrote to parents, knowing that they would have genuine concerns about such a risky activity. The kids and I discussed how their parents would need time to learn more about the trip. We talked about how we could best inform parents and obtain permission for everyone to go. Soon after, Clearwater Sports generously offered its support in equipment and two experienced guides. At the school open house, I garnered enough parent volunteers to put one adult and two kids in each canoe.

I lay awake in bed the morning of the trip, listening to the wind and rain on the roof. I wondered if I was taking too big a risk with this trip. I was very nervous. After talking with the kids, chaperones, and Clearwater, however, we decided we were well prepared and ready to accept the challenge. We had spent time receiving dry-land instruction, and we were well equipped with extra clothes and food in dry bags. The weather was damp and cold that late October day, but our spirits were high. Six hours later, we had accumulated a wonderful collection of memories.

At the first set of rapids, one of the canoes got caught sideways on a rock, and my fear of a capsizing was realized. Danny, sitting too high, took a plunge into the chilly waters. The life jacket supported him, and the canoe tugged him safely to shore. Danny's biggest concern was where to find an appropriate place to change while preserving his modesty. Soon he found a private spot, changed into dry clothes, and was ready to continue. In this situation, my young adolescents learned from another kid's mistake. From then on, they knelt on the floor of the canoes as they'd been instructed. Our caravan of canoes traveled on, more respectful of the river's dangers.

Why Me?

There they were, our first set of rapids. A shiver of excitement rushed through me. The canoe with Shane's, Dad's, and my help moved toward the rough water. We moved with ease through the first part of the rapids. Then, ever so gradually we began to turn sideways. In a time span of two seconds we were sideways. We hit a rock. Shane and I panicked and leaned. My heart jumped into my throat. Shane saved the canoe by gallantly hurling his arm into the whirling rapids and pushing the canoe into an upright stance. The jolt threw me off balance and I was plunged into the foaming rapids.

I was going to die, I thought, as I hit the water. Killed-gonzo-annihilated. Going over a small waterfall brought me back to my senses. I tried to breathe but instead I took in water. I left the rapids with many questions. Should I let the current take me downstream or go to the canoe, or . . . ? Then I saw the canoe was sideways. It couldn't get to me, I had to get to it. I started taking in gasps of air but only a little could get through my lungs. I, for the first time in a long time, was really scared. Much to my surprise, I saw the canoe coming toward me. I was going to be okay. I felt like crying.

Danny Senning

After a portage around the Middlesex Dam and lunch, we started off again. Junkyard Rapids was our next obstacle. We landed our canoes upstream and walked out onto a rock overlooking the white water, selecting the best path to take. Our guide startled us by noting that he had flipped there a few times. Then, following our guides, each canoe successfully tackled the rapids one by one and took out on the downstream shore to cheers of joy and accomplishment.

Being part of the river, we all learned so much that day—about listening and following instructions, about canoeing, about observing wildlife, about the flow of the river, about teamwork, but mostly about ourselves. Students' writings clearly reflected their insights.

The Rapids of Fury

I could hear the whooshing of the water as Andy Ripley, Nathan Apolito, and I approached the fury of the Junkyard Rapids. The fear of flipping sent a chill up my spine!

The canoe bobbed up and down as we began to paddle very carefully. Suddenly, as if sucked into a vacuum cleaner, we were pulled into the currents.

I shivered with fear when we were in the middle of the rapids. I stuck my head down between my knees as we dodged the only rock that was in the way.

With a deep sigh, I began to cheer, for we had conquered the Junkyard Rapids. Now I felt that, whatever was in front of us, would always be conquered. I felt great!

Jason Blake

My favorite activity was the canoe trip. I say this because for one day I was part of the river. Not just someone on the banks or someone who was passing by. I was part of the river.

D. S.

My favorite activity was the canoe trip because we were on the river and got the full sense of what the river was really like. We got to paddle and work as a team going through the rapids. I also learned a lot, being that I had never canoed before and that it was a new experience for me.

B. T.

STUDENT-CENTERED LEARNING

How do I assess the learning that occurred during the river unit? With the journals we'd kept, the writing we'd polished, the photographs I'd taken, and the folders of information we'd collected, we already had much documentation. We used it all as a foundation.

I listed all the activities we had experienced and asked students to rank them according to their learning value. A compilation of these data was the basis for a valuable class interview of what worked, what didn't, and why. This discussion and individual student journals became the starting point for a major learning statement. In an essay, students responded to four questions:

1. What did you learn during the river study?
2. What was your favorite activity and why?
3. What did you learn about others during the unit?
4. What did you learn about yourself and how you learn?

I found this to be a very valuable way to better understand my students and their learning.

It's Time to Go With the Flow

1. This river study was a great learning experience for me. I never thought I would be doing things like piloting a canoe, watching sewage being cleaned, finding animal tracks and making them into plaster models, walking on the Winooski delta, walking across the Waterbury Dam, building a mini-raft, and much, much more. It was great!

2. My favorite learning experience has to be the canoe trip. Learning how to paddle and everything was hard, but fun. I learned that you really have to keep your balance, or you're going to flip. J. B. and I almost did.

3. It's kind of hard to understand, but I learned the most about my own mother. Every night I would come and tell her what we had done on the river study that day. She would always act weird, like the whole thing was stupid. When she got to go on the canoe trip with us, I found that all of her acting had been from jealousy.

4. During this river study, I had never thought about it, but I have been learning to understand myself. I've found that I learn better if I stop fooling around with the guys, and get right down to business. Sometimes, Treavor & Co. will say, "Have some fun, don't take it so seriously." Then I want to fool around again. But if I really think about it, it's better to learn. It's fun, too.

Nathan Apolito

My Experiences With Life

1. What I learned about the river was that it has moods. At times the river is fierce, but at other times it is calm and understanding. The river is a symbol, it is a symbol of life. Without the river there would be no life.

2. My favorite part of the river unit was when we made our mind maps, but I have another favorite part, and that was the final test, because the class got to make their own questions.

3. There are a few people who taught me a lesson for life, but Danny taught me the most. Danny isn't the kind of person that once you're down, you stay down. When Danny fell out of the canoe he didn't panic, he didn't start screaming, he just grabbed onto the canoe and let it pull him to shore. When he got onto the shore he was ready to go on in his wet clothes but we gave him dry ones to change into.

I learned that I can learn a lot of things from old people. Older people are usually wiser and know more because they've been around longer. I also learned that older people can learn stuff from younger people about the new stuff like rock and roll, and what's in style.

4. I learned that I can be sensible at times even though I like to fool around. I also learned that if you want to be number one, you've got to work for it, you can't just sit back and watch the birds fly by.

Treavor Clark

I asked the students to review their folders to create a final concept map that explained in as much detail as possible the seven aspects of the river that we had explored. Then seven small groups were formed to create a list of test questions for each area.

The class busily took notes while each group reported their questions and discussed possible answers. I selected questions from each group for a final test. I found the questions to be of excellent quality and often more difficult than I would have asked. Their questions and their performance on this test reflected the magnitude of their learning throughout the river study.

One day somewhere in the middle of the unit, we were playing with words, using water and river idioms and deciding on a title for what we were doing: On the Waterfront, Hold Your Water, Up the Creek With(out) a Paddle, Wet and Wild, Staying Current, Go With the Flow.

Go With the Flow, which I had hit upon during my summer planning, best fit what was really happening with our class study. The kids agreed because they could see how the joint planning had flowed nicely into the activities. One activity had led into the next one. Connections between activities were fluid. They realized that sometimes our mood in the unit shifted like the changing moods of the river. Some days we rushed madly ahead; other days we floated along placidly. As we continued, we made some mistakes and missed some opportunities for further study. But that's exactly what happens when we're traveling on a river. And our Winooski River journey was a great learning adventure!

Chapter 11

Climb Every Mountain

Ann Reames, Chris Gorman, and Keith Pillsbury
Essex Middle School, Essex Town

The anticipation was high! The clothing was layered! The daypacks were heavy! The cameras were loaded! The mountain was . . . *in clouds.* A difficult decision confronted us.

"If I were 11 years old, climbing the mountain today would not be much fun. It's cloudy and cool up here," said our friendly meteorologist at the station at the top of Mount Mansfield in response to our last-minute telephone call. What's the point of going if you can't see anything? So . . . *unlayer, unpack, unload.*

The delay of our planned hike to the top of Mount Mansfield was just another glitch in developing our very first team-taught integrated study. Morale sank to a new low that morning for students and teachers alike. It took us back to our sometimes frustrated beginnings.

Four months earlier, we three teachers had participated in a course on integrated study in the middle grades, providing our first opportunity to work together as a team. That work had left us both apprehensive and excited about the coming year, the changes we would be undertaking, and our ability to work successfully and amicably together for a whole year.

Our first idea had been to develop a study on the topic of survival, a focus that would encompass all of the characteristics of a good integrated study. However, dealing with such a comprehensive, potentially grim topic gave us fits, starts, and sleepless nights. Our conceptualization of the topic was simply too broad and unfocused for us to work with. But soon, a possible activity we had listed on our planning web captured our enthusiasm, and we were off and running. The mountain we had seen and taken for granted every day for years now became the focus of our energies. Mount Mansfield is an isolated mountain in the Green Mountain range that has a unique ridge line that appears to have characteristics of a human face. It dominates the eastern view from the town where we teach. Aha! Our new team had survived its first curriculum crisis!

Six weeks later, the summer was over and we launched our study—sort of. "Where is it?" exclaimed the bus driver and 60 other inquiring minds as the large yellow bus pulled into the Martin's supermarket parking lot, a perfect vantage point from which to view and sketch the Mount Mansfield profile that suggested the face of a man. Unfortunately, the mountain creates its own weather patterns, and on this particular day, the "man" was in the clouds (and not for the last time, we were later to learn). One student wrote:

> The mountain makes me feel mad because I can hardly see it. The clouds and trees are blocking my view.

Turning this disappointment into something valuable, we sketched the horizon and urged kids to express their mood through creative writing.

> The mountains are peaceful and soft. They represent freedom and stubbornness. The blue clouds and light yellow sunlight blend together to make it look silent, but it still speaks for itself. "Listen," it says, "You are yourself and you can do it."
>
> *Sara*

The following day, we used the webbing technique we had learned in the summer with our students to establish what they already knew plus what they wanted to learn more about. Bekah's web is one example of that work (see Figure 11.1).

Energy was contagious, and kids' ideas seemed to be limitless. They were ready to study our mountain.

One thing everyone wanted to do was climb the mountain, but we

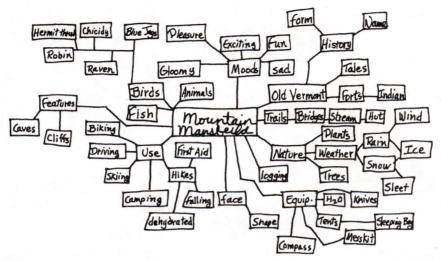

Figure 11.1. Bekah's web.

were well into autumn. Snow and ice could arrive abruptly at any time, making the trek risky. Nevertheless, we plunged into planning the trip. For many of our students, climbing the mountain became a symbol for overcoming challenges and reaching a goal. Committees were formed to make preparations. Students became experts in first aid, photography, nature, trail food, weather, and equipment. They began searching for answers to their questions about the hike:

> How cold will it be?
> What will I eat?
> What should I wear?
> What are the dangers?

It had truly become their hike, therefore bringing personal meaning to their work and learning.

The students also shared their expertise with each other. They speculated about how long it would take to make the climb. It seemed advisable that they should establish three different climbing groups: a fast group, a moderate group, and a leisurely group. After making a choice about which climbing group to join, they were ready for the hike. The big day had come: We dealt with disappointment, and that day passed. The *next* Friday would surely be our big day.

Well, I feel good. It would not have been much fun because we would not be able to see any views or any other mountains. It would be dangerous, too, because we would not be able to see very far in the fog! I can only hope for good weather next Friday.

Pat H.

I feel real mad that we could not go on Mount Mansfield. . . . One thing I feel real mad [about] is that I have [on] some uncomfortable long underwear.

Pat R.

During the intervening week, we worked in study groups based on themes rather than on curriculum areas: tourism and other industries, nature of the mountain, legends, and the arts. Students collected leaves, studied the ski industry, designed posters of the four seasons, illustrated Robert Frost poems, identified trees, wrote journal entries, and lots more. One particularly rewarding project was making a mural that represented the changes in the mountain environment that we could see along the climb.

The big day finally came *again!* One teacher wrote:

When I woke up this morning and peered into the darkness, I wasn't sure still if we had made the right decision last Friday. But as the sun came up and I could see that it was at least partly clear, I was very excited. On the way into work I experienced a really elated feeling about living in such a beautiful place and having a job that can be so rewarding. The morning was picture perfect. The top 1/3 of the mountain was all frosty and the bottom 2/3 was all color. I just knew we were going to have a tremendous day!

Excitement was again high, layered clothing was once again the order of the day, the daypacks were still heavy, and the cameras remained loaded and ready. In a flash we were off, and what a fabulous time we had!

I found that my group liked to stop a lot. Tracy had to stop to take medicine for asthma; Betsy stopped for side aches; Mrs. Gorman breaked for water and Kleenex; and I stopped to rest my ankle. We were at a leisurely pace and enjoyed ourselves. We all like the man-made bridges. The most memorable part of the day was eating lunch on the very large rock. Mrs. Gorman was scared that we would fall off the edge so she sat on the side. We ate lunch and slid down.

Bekah

A memorable sight I saw was the snow. From a rock we were standing on we could see the different kinds of trees and when you look high enough you can see snow. A girl in my group said it was a painter's paradise.

Betsy

I learned that I was afraid (scared) of real steep edges. I feel we all have our own pace and mine is moderate. My pace may be slower than others, but I learned to keep your pace, don't try to catch up with others; they'll wait for you.

Riann

I learned that I get cold very easily and that I can go a long time without eating. I learned that I really enjoy the mountains and I really push myself up and down things with my right leg. I learned that I am really, really afraid of heights.

Jennifer

I learned that hiking can be a lot of fun, especially with friends and your dad. . . . I think lunch was the most memorable part of the trip because I loved how we were just sitting around talking, laughing, and taking pictures. My dad and I plan to blow up the picture of all of us and have it copied for each of us . . . and be able to have them as posters.

Julie

I learned that teachers can be a lot of fun, and I also learned that if you and other people work together you can accomplish more.

Betsy

Back in our classroom the following Monday, we had several discussions about what it meant to do one's personal best. Then all the energy centered on project work being done in groups. This piece of the study was based entirely on students' choice from an array of ideas that had been generated through brainstorming. A number of students developed games around a mountain theme, such as "Mountopoly" and "Surprise Mountain." The *Mountain Press* newspaper evolved from the study, as did an original song, "The Mountain Song," and a futuristic plan, Juleen's Ski Lodge. Models, paintings, graphs, and data bases were created, shared, and displayed. Students found that working in small groups had advantages and disadvantages.

It is very difficult to work with another person. Jeanine didn't want a comment page, but I did, but she got her way anyway. We worked hard on this book of poems and stories.

Devon

I learned that when I'm in a group I can work pretty well. 'Cause we had to do our project all over again and we did it pretty fast. I also learned that I should never put my projects on the floor. And I'm glad that Mr. Pillsbury told us that it was destroyed. 'Cause if we had just walked in there and seen it, we would have been shocked.

Derek

There was standing room only when slides were shown to our 60 students' families at our team's open house. Our guests experienced the climb up Sunset Ridge through their own children's and other students' eyes. Parents browsed among displays of the various projects as the students talked about what they had learned.

But what had they truly learned? The next step was assessment. Students completed self-evaluation forms. We graded their project presentations and conferenced about a final grade for the unit. Although academics were part of the learning experience, we also wanted students to learn and practice the social skills of cooperation and positive communication. Also stressed throughout the unit was the importance of meeting challenges by doing one's personal best. An entry from one of our own journals provided valuable assessment information:

It always surprises me when I hike in the East. Why don't they use more switchbacks on the trails? Sunset Ridge is a fairly easy trail, but it has been heavily used for many years. Erosion has worn the trail away to bedrock. The rocks had fallen leaves and snow on them the day we climbed, which made some spots tricky. I could tell that some of the students felt at home scrambling up those slippery rocks like monkeys. And some didn't.

One particularly revealing incident that I think will always stick with me involved a homeroom student named Rick. Rick is a withdrawn boy who avoided interaction with his peers in most settings. He was climbing the mountain with a parent-led group of 4 or 5 boys. At one point during the trip my group caught up with their group. When I saw what was happening, I kept the hikers in my group from moving ahead because I knew Rick would be embarrassed if a crowd witnessed his predicament.

Rick had encountered a particularly slippery, steep set of rocks and had given up. He was lying in the trail, crying and saying that he wanted to go back. The boys in Rick's group offered encouragement without gawking, and the father who was the group leader was a joy to watch. He coaxed, cajoled, explained, and promised. After about 10 minutes, I offered Rick the chance to head back down the mountain, but the rest of the boys cheered him on and he decided to keep going.

I didn't see Rick again during the hike, but when we returned to the bottom, I learned that his group had reached the summit. We were all very proud of Rick.

The important part of this story is the change we all saw in Rick after this experience. He had made some connections with his peers. He had found some success, and he was more friendly and talkative with other kids. His self-confidence was improved through this experience, and he opened up to all of us. I don't pretend to think that it was the mountain experience alone that caused the change, but the success Rick experienced sure didn't hurt!

We've agreed that the next time we undertake this study, we will increase the number of days for study groups, increase what we call kidaccountability by having students make up test questions, and work to improve the use of journals.

We were pleased with our many successes. Our major goals were achieved. The unit was balanced with activities that ranged from no choice to unlimited choice. We believe the study successfully met the needs of our students in this particular setting. It gave them the opportunity to socialize and to learn how to cooperate with each other. They also grew more adept at solving a variety of problems. Our students learned how to plan activities, and they learned to work well in groups, sharing responsibility for collecting data. And especially important to us, they became much more aware and appreciative of our mountain.

It's soft,
Barely heard
It's a mountain
everyone
Young and old
Trying to
Be better than
The soft,
Lonely,
Scarcely ever seen
Mountain.
The mountain's peaks of
Purple and gold
Reach as high as you can
Reach, mountain
Reach some more
Tell the people
Who never listen
Tell them to listen
Listen to the soft,
Glowing, courageous
Thing, we call a mountain.

Sara

V

INTEREST STUDIES

Chapter 12

The Big Alpha Circus

Carol Smith, Barbara Blaise, Linda Mann, and David Myers

Shelburne Middle School, Shelburne

> Ladieees aaand gentlemen!
> Boys and girls, chiiillldren of all ages . . .

The circus brought back childhood memories for each of us, recollections with temptations we couldn't resist. It was a part of our past, and because of the Big Apple Circus' annual visit to our town, it was part of our present as well. The circus was a living illustration of teamwork, cultural diversity, and individual excellence. Rich in history and tradition, it was relevant, extravagant, and exciting—a perfect topic for interdisciplinary study by students on our multiage team.

Our circus study became the focus of a summer interdisciplinary curriculum course for two teachers on the Alpha team, Linda Mann and Carol Smith, joined by physical education teacher Barbara Blaise and instrumental music director David Myers. Although this would not be the Alpha program's first integrated unit, it marked our first effort with teachers from outside our team.

BREAKING GROUND

The week-long institute was merely the beginning—the easing into what soon became a roller coaster ride we couldn't (and wouldn't) get off. We worked on a general outline for our fall study and divided up tasks for the remainder of the summer.

Friends thought we were crazy, and our families listened politely to circus lore (and gore) each night at the dinner table. Prime tanning time was spent at the library instead of at the lake. We wrote letters to faraway places like Venice and Baraboo.

And then the circus came to town. It was August, it was hot, and it was early in the morning, well before first light. By truck, van, and 18-wheeler, the Big Apple Circus began rolling in. And we were there in summer heat watching the circus come to life in Shelburne. We photographed everything and talked to anyone who would stand still. We watched, we listened, and we waited.

Finally, the tent went up. It took 60 to 70 people working together in careful coordination to raise that big top . . . and it worked. A shiny white tent with big red stars transformed the drab parking lot into a place of wonder. Concession stands went up, and workers hurried to get ready. Excitement began to brew, and we knew why we had waited. The Big Apple Circus brought our reading and research to life.

Early in the summer, we had sent Alpha students a flyer inviting them to "run away with the circus." A wealth of circus activities had been scheduled by the nearby Shelburne Museum, and we outlined them for students and invited them to participate. All during our week on location, we bumped into students who asked:

Are we really going to study the circus?
What's there to study?
Can I be the clown?

Some students took advantage of circus activities almost daily. There were sessions with the elephant trainer, clown workshops, back-lot tours, and open ringside rehearsals. Everywhere we went, we found our students as well. They had begun to catch our excitement.

Several seventh and eighth graders accepted our invitation to help us interview and videotape. Vanessa, a circus performer we interviewed, spoke about her move from the Ringling Bros. Barnum & Bailey Circus to the smaller, more theatrical atmosphere of the Big Apple, where she felt she was an integral part of the whole circus operation. "It's a family," she said, "a community that lives and works together, sharing in the successes and supporting each other when there's fail-ure." She surprised us by telling us that she was a college graduate who, after getting her degree, "ran away with the circus."

Krista remarked later, "I thought everyone in the circus was born there. I didn't know people would just choose it for a job."

We and our students also spent time with the teacher from the cir-cus' One Ring Schoolhouse. She taught nine students aged 3 through 14 all together in the One Ring Schoolhouse, which was in reality a small pop-up camper. She talked about using the community as a resource for her teaching. "Because the circus moves to so many var-ied locations, using the local resources in each community adds a rich-ness not found in texts," she told us. "It's more real. The children are here in this place, and learning about it makes the learning real." Krista and Kirsten exchanged a look that said, "We know about that. We're here learning about you."

All in all, we spent a week at the circus, immersing ourselves in its wonder. We had an inside look into a different world, and the excite-ment spread. We reaffirmed our knowledge that striving for excellence was at the very center of circus philosophy, just as striving for excel-lence was our goal in Alpha as well. By September, we were ready to create a circus extravaganza of our own.

BACKLOT TOUR

Our study was to focus on three elements of the circus: the history, bringing the circus to town, and the performance. We had planned to devote a week to each section and then spend the last 2 weeks totally immersed in planning our own Big Alpha Circus. It became apparent early on that activities and assessments associated with the beginning of the year would need to be completed before we could begin the unit, so our study had to be pushed back. We had chosen a date in mid-October for our class performance, and despite the delay, we needed to meet that commitment.

SETTING THE STAGE

It was important to have students involved from the beginning in the planning of the actual study. In part, the Alpha philosophy states that "students and teachers are partners in learning and must participate together in the learning process, establishing programs and setting goals that best reflect the needs and interests of each individual." With time at a premium, it became necessary to rethink total student involvement at each step in the planning process. Again, we enlisted the leadership and help of our seventh and eighth graders. After a whole class of brainstorming in which we identified aspects of the circus, these students categorized the topics and, together with teachers, did preliminary research on topics ranging from sideshows and circus "freaks" to daredevils and clowns. This general information was presented to the rest of the class, and then seventh and eighth graders worked with small groups of students to discover what they already knew and what they wanted to find out.

Christina wrote in her journal:

> I liked working with the younger kids. It gave me a chance to try out being a leader.

Sam reflected:

> Working with the teachers to help plan our study was fun. They listened to what I thought. It felt good.

At daily class meetings, the excitement grew as we began to talk about possibilities for our own circus. We talked about clowns and acrobats, fat ladies and strongmen, lions and elephants. Some worried that we couldn't get an elephant; others began to imagine ways we could. "With the right costume and balanced on one foot on a stool, someone could look like an elephant. That's what all elephants do. People would recognize the idea of it. I'll be the elephant," Bobby offered. The dream of the Big Alpha Circus took root.

OUTSIDE THE RING

In these beginning weeks, our circus study was sprinkled throughout the day. We incorporated activities whenever possible while we went about the business of beginning a new school year. Each student designed a circus wagon car, complete with his or her idea of the most important aspect of the circus. Soon, lions and elephants, clowns and acrobats, horses and daredevils of all kinds paraded around the perimeter of our four classrooms.

We were also able to take advantage of circus memorabilia housed at the nearby Shelburne Museum. Field trips there offered all students the chance to experience the golden age of circuses through the museum's many artifacts, especially its extensive collection of posters. Other required class activities included listening to traditional circus music, examining authentic circus posters, honing skills for writing a friendly (fan) letter, and reviewing how to use reference books to locate information. Circus history was brought to life by an extensive collection of films. After watching a movie on Clown College, Andrea reported that:

> All clowns have to create their own character, makeup, and costume. They have to create an original gimmick. I think I'll be a clown who walks on stilts.

Special guests were invited to share their circus skills. We discovered a mime (disguised as a speech pathologist) right in our own Shelburne Middle School. Another friend walked on stilts. Students were required to attend these special presentations, but other requirements became more individualized: choosing a circus research topic, creating a circus act, keeping a journal, designing an advertising poster.

Outside the Alpha classrooms, other circus activities began to take shape. Judy Kelly, our art teacher, began a unit on figures in flight. The final products were an assortment of almost life-size papier-mâché aerialists flying with the greatest of ease through the school lobby. Cindy Myers, our living arts teacher, helped kids to design a logo for the Big Alpha Circus, which they brought back for the whole team's critique and subsequent approval. They went about the business of silk-screening T-shirts for Alpha students and for others who wished to purchase one. Physical education classes began to focus on tumbling, rhythm, and dance. Juggling was introduced, and gymnastics was encouraged. Circus music was our constant classroom companion, and language expressions emphasizing alliteration became part of our speech. Circus wagon bulletin boards housing lions, monkeys, and bears rolled through the library. Everywhere there were signs of the circus.

GETTING OUR ACT TOGETHER

It was our original expectation that every child would participate in the performance of the Big Alpha Circus. Not all students wished to share the spotlight in the ring, however. Individual interests were evident as sideshow operators, vendors, roustabouts, and concession stand entrepreneurs emerged. We had a video crew, lighting crew, and ticket taker. Very soon, the image of "star" took on new meaning as students began to see and understand, through experience, the relationship between the parts and the whole.

Erika said, "The sound and smell of popcorn popping would really add to the circus atmosphere."

Tyler asked, "What would the circus be without balloons?"

Gena questioned, "Can I help organize a sideshow? I have some ideas for creating 'freaks' without hurting anyone's feelings."

Ben suggested, "A filler act could distract the attention of the audience while the ring crew does its job."

Sam boasted, "If I figured this right, cotton candy will be a real money-maker."

As life-size papier-mâché acrobats began to take shape in the art room, real-life acrobats practiced in the gym. Clown faces were designed, and costumes took shape. Props were made, and music was selected. The sideshow began to take shape. Concession stand operators decided on a product, researched the costs involved, and began their advertising campaigns. Vendors rented equipment and put the finishing touches on their red-striped vests.

Practice began, and practice continued day after day. David Myers met with a group of students to work out the design and the logistics of a tent and a circus ring. Teachers arrived early and stayed late. We ate lunch to circus music. We calmed nerves, dried tears, and settled disputes. We laughed and applauded in all the right places (and in some not-so-right places), prompting revision and fine-tuning. We juggled entrances and exits. We practiced the parade and synchronized the music. We created simple filler acts to draw the audience's attention while the ring crew did its work. And it all began to come together.

RAISING THE BIG TOP

Our team of roustabouts consisted of 6 adults and 12 students. A brightly colored parachute was to be our tent, and folded gym mats bordered our ring. Those charged with staging measured and remeasured. A pulley system was attached, and those of us designated as ballast stood ready. We braced, and they pulled. They tightened. We held. They tied and knotted, and we held and held until finally the Big Alpha Circus big top was up!

A transformed fireplace prop from the previous year's musical show provided an entryway, and colorful banners hid waiting performers. Bright crepe paper streamers dipped out and down from the parachute, creating the illusion of a huge tent. Staging two stories high held our eight sets of lights, cable, and video equipment. Four hundred chairs sat empty around our ring. We dimmed the house lights, turned up the spot, and stared at each other in awe. An illusion had become a reality!

THE BIG ALPHA CIRCUS

7:00 PM: The doors opened. Papier-mâché acrobats swung through the lobby, greeting parents and guests. Colorful posters promised exciting and fabulous acts to come: the Ferocious Felines, Hermie the Magnificent, the Golden Ravens.

A contortionist stared blankly from her glass box as the hyena laughed hysterically. An ostrich sang opera while strongmen strained under their barbells. Gypsy Siamese twins enticed those who dared into their fortune-telling parlor, and the fat man was "out to lunch." The aroma of popcorn, caramel apples, and cotton candy drew people to the concession area, where operators in red-striped vests barked their wares. Balloon vendors on stilts circled the circus ring as adults and children found their seats under the big top.

The house lights dimmed, and the ringmaster stepped into the spotlight: "Ladieees aaand gentlemen! Boys and girls, chiiillldren of all ages! Where fantasy becomes reality and imagination reigns supreme—the Big Alpha Circus!"

Fatigue fell away as we were swept up in the fantasy we had created together. Greasepaint, costumes, and wigs had transformed our students into clowns, snakes, polar bears, tigers, elephants, and yes, the teachers into French poodles. We had mime artists, acrobats, highwire performers, and slack-wire stars. We had clowns, jugglers, magicians, tumblers, stilt walkers, wild animals, and wild animal trainers. There were the Terrific Tumbling Trio, the Rhythmic Ribbon Twirlers, Clown Around Currie, Mime Magic, Schaharazade, Dr. Dooker, Binky and Bonzo Bear, FiFi, FuFu, MiMi, and LuLu.

We laughed. The kids laughed. The audience laughed. And they roared their applause. A standing ovation greeted the Big Alpha Circus troupe as they paraded one last time around the ring, waving, smiling, glowing.

It was over in a heartbeat. The tent came down quickly, and the glitter was swept away. Faces were scrubbed clean, and props headed for storage. What the Big Apple Circus had done for us as teachers, the Big Alpha Circus had done for our kids. As they wrote afterward:

Everybody loves the circus!
Our circus was successful because everyone chose their personal contribution. We each had our own spotlight.
Our tent was terrific . . . we created the perfect illusion.
Improvisation was how we fixed our "mistakes."
We had to work together, we even had to compromise.
The circus blends history and traditions from all over the world.
Studying the circus never left time for being bored.
The circus is a family. . . . It was perfect for Alpha.

Our circus study truly brought learning to life. Its success relied on cooperation and teamwork and demanded individual effort as well. No job was too small, and all skills had value. Every child stood for a moment in the spotlight—each one applauded, each one a star.

Chapter 13

Inventions

Nancy Phillips, Suzanne Dirmaier, and Heidi Ringer
Warren Elementary School, Warren

Equipped with diet soda, three flavors of gum, markers of various colors, and a brand-new pad of chart paper, we began the first planning session for our new team's first-ever integrated study, a study of inventions and inventing. We wanted to take advantage of our 10- to 12-year-old students' natural processes of imagination, which are evident when they create a toy, invent a playmate, or concoct ingenious ways of getting out of unpleasant chores.

We had heard about an exhibit of Leonardo da Vinci's inventions at the Musée de Beaux Arts in nearby Montreal. We knew that some good units of study had evolved from meaningful field trips in the past, so we contemplated the possibilities for a study of inventions. A field trip to the da Vinci exhibit emerged as a central part of our overall plan.

First, we took turns brainstorming and sharing ideas about what each of us believed was important to include in this unit. We needed to distinguish between what we wanted to teach and what we wanted our 10-, 11-, and 12-year-olds to gain from their study. We listed ideas that we probably would not be able to get to in 4 weeks, but it was important that we shared them and listed them on paper. Our process of imagining possibilities established the same kind of climate we wanted the children to experience.

This particular unit constituted the very first time that our new team of three had worked together. Although Suzanne and Nancy had worked at the school together for quite a few years, they had never taught a unit together. Heidi was entirely new to the team. This project would be our first collaboration as the upper unit team. It was the first test of our ability to work together, and we happily discovered through this project that we work together very well.

Our brainstorming identified ideas that connected to specific subject areas: Math and science were clearly linked to the technical realm; music and art reflected expressive dimensions. We wanted each student to invest some portion of each day learning about different aspects of inventions.

Next, we established a time line, arranging schedules for everything from our whole group introductions to a boat-building project to free-choice activities to each child's presentation of his or her own invention. Our final activity would be a field trip to Montreal. These activities fit beautifully on paper into 18 fun-filled school days, but the reality of the children working their way through our plan was another time line altogether.

Once we had finished our planning session, we posted around the room the chart that clustered the ideas we'd decided to include, a beautiful time line, and an activity chart that indicated which one of us would do which activity. We believed that dividing the responsibility for specific activities among us would make teaching this unit much more reasonable and complete. We felt very satisfied with the work we had done during this planning session, and we were now ready to put our plan into action.

CHILDREN'S IDEAS

The first step was to explore the concept of invention by having the children work in small groups to think of examples of inventions and inventors and to create a list of inventors and inventions. Each group wrote its own definition and compiled its own list. Our main purpose was to ensure that the children understood and could explain the definition. After the small-group brainstorming sessions, the children came back together to share their work. We listed their definitions on chart paper. Using everyone's work, the whole group then decided on a definition that most accurately defined the word. This negotiation turned out to be the easiest part of the process. Next, we went through the list of inventors to decide if they belonged in the category of inventor. This collaboration brought forth lively discussions. Some of the questions students wrestled with during this brainstorming activity were:

Is Stephen Spielberg an inventor?
Is Judy Blume an inventor?
Is Kentucky Fried Chicken an invention?
Is the Barbie doll an invention?
Is God an inventor?

HOPAMEBOATAFLOATA REGATTA

The next aspect of the unit was the Hopameboatafloata Regatta, a problem-solving activity that Heidi had learned in a summer teachers' institute. The children had to invent a boat that fit certain specifications: no longer than 12 inches, no wider than 4 inches, and with a total sail area of no more than 40 square inches. The boat had to sail downwind in a shallow rectangular pond we built in the classroom, using a window fan for wind power. This activity involved kids in the process of building a sailboat to specifications, testing it, changing it, testing it again, and continuing the process as long as necessary until they had a boat they thought would at least survive the race if not win it.

Lake Hopameboatafloata was constructed by first using 2 x 6 planks to build a wooden frame 10 feet long and 4 feet wide. With this box resting on the floor of a covered porch outside our gym, we lined the frame with a large sheet of heavy-grade plastic—creating a tub we could fill with a garden hose. Luckily, we were near a water source—it took a while to fill the lake, and we had to top it off every few days because of evaporation. To finish the lake, we stapled the overhanging plastic to the frame and placed a 24-inch window fan at one end so that the breeze would sweep evenly across the water surface.

The lake was set up on the day the children received their instructions, so they had a place to experiment with from the beginning. We also stimulated their thinking by bringing in lots of boat ideas. Some children assumed that they had to build a boat to look like a boat. Then some sample boats were made from a mushroom crate, tinfoil, and styrofoam—stimulating more imagination. It was important for us to continually encourage some children to keep trying and seeking solutions to their problems.

Throughout the trial races, they learned that their great ideas had to be worked out. Their journals revealed their insights and their consternation over the simple realization that "Elmer's glue doesn't stick when it gets wet" or "Well, today my boat sank and it's back to the worktable." Max, who was determined to win, summarized, "It just didn't go fast enough." Sarah's writing revealed her grasp of the complexity of her boat's development: "My boat didn't stay up, so I had to put more weight on one side and put a keel on to make it go straight."

We had to revise our rules when we recognized that some children required more guidance than others. We also tried to eliminate problems that might arise from parental help by establishing two distinct categories: the Kids' Cup (without adult help) and the Kids' Cup Plus (with adult help). Most children chose to build their own boats, as the following journal entries indicate:

> I wanted to learn to build my own boat. People can't do everything for me.

> I wanted to do it alone because I would learn more about myself.

Others who felt they needed a little extra help or perhaps had the desire to win wrote:

> I did my boat mostly with help, because I knew I would lose if I built it myself.

On the day of the big race, the children entered one of the two categories. Then they paired off within these groups. The race was based on elimination rounds, and the winners of each heat were randomly paired again. The heats continued until we had first, second, and third place winners in each category.

Suzanne kept charge of winners, handling the pairings and keeping the school news media informed. Heidi was in charge of starting each heat and making judgment calls in case of protest. Nancy helped judge the finishes while she videotaped the entire event to share later with parents. The children cheered all the boats, making everyone a winner as they heard classmates chanting for them and their entries. We concluded with an awards ceremony in which winners were photographed holding their boats and wearing their Hopameboatafloata Regatta buttons. All participants were applauded for their enthusiasm, cooperation, and fair play.

It was a special joy to read in one student's journal that the essence of the regatta had come across:

> My process in building my boat was to build, test, improve, test, improve . . . or in my case rebuild when your boat sinks.

With the spirit of this thought in mind, we were on to our next activity, which would help lay additional steps in the process of inventing.

RUBE GOLDBERG

Our next step in the process of inventing was another structured activity centered on the comic strip created by Rube Goldberg. Goldberg's imaginary character, Professor Butts, created timesaving inventions that used a series of chain reactions to do a simple job such as switching on or off a light switch. These inventions usually took longer and were more elaborate than just walking over and flipping the switch, usually taking 10 steps to do it. However, the chain reactions were interesting to the children, and they reflected just the kind of imaginative thinking we wanted them to express.

Students were introduced to the concept of chain reactions through a hands-on activity using dominoes. They had to set up their dominoes so that when the first domino tipped over, the rest would follow in succession. This was a very lively activity, and children created several different chain reactions, each one more complicated than the previous one.

Next, we wanted the children to create their own Rube Goldberg chain reaction pictures. First, students pasted together a series of pictures to create an invention that turned something on through a series of comical disjointed events (I stepped on the cat, which chased the mouse, which ran into the cage, and so on, until the light was finally turned on). Then students created their own Rube Goldberg-like cartoons.

During this activity, we introduced the process of critiquing each other's work in order to get additional ideas for the cartoons. As teachers, we concentrated on modeling to teach the children how to phrase their suggestions in a positive manner. For most children, this was an important part of the activity because it helped them to solve their problems and gave them new ideas about how to make their projects better. We also believed this was a real-life situation that inventors experience when they work on a project.

SURVEYS

With the children's participation, we created a survey that they took home to ask their parents or older relatives what the most important inventions and scientific breakthroughs were that occurred when they were children aged 9 to 12. We believed it was important for the children to have a personal sense of what their parents thought were important inventions during their childhood.

We helped the students to compile their information into decades—prior to 1940, the 1940s, the 1950s, and the 1960s. If the resource person had been a child during the 1950s, his or her information was listed under that heading. Afterwards, we analyzed the results. A conspicuous trend throughout the decades was the evolution of air travel from the first airplane ride to a man in space and, finally, the first moon landing. Other scientific breakthroughs centered around medicine. Although much of this information could have been found in the encyclopedia, we saw that the firsthand experience of collecting and using knowledge from home made it all much more meaningful to students. They had tallied parents' ideas and drawn conclusions—a more effective learning experience for them than just looking something up in a book.

The students also surveyed themselves about the three inventions that were most important to them and what inventions were still needed. We thought they should see what their own peers believed was important. Younger children felt the teddy bear was an important invention, and the other children were inclined toward the telephone and the television as most important. The last part of the survey—what needed to be invented—was used to introduce the next activity, Create Your Own Invention.

CREATE YOUR OWN INVENTION

This activity began by having kids identify things that they thought needed to be invented. Their ideas were especially interesting. Each age group seemed to have a common need.

We hoped the ideas from the discussion would provide some starting places for ideas for an invention. For some children, the idea of creating an invention seemed like a huge task, while others met the challenge eagerly. Mary wrote, "They told us today about the inventions. I am doomed." Bob was more cavalier, "The only problem I had was thinking of an invention." And Susan had the task all wrapped up: "This is going to be fun. I am going to invent a new toothbrush."

Next, we selected readings from Stephen Caney's *The Invention Handbook* to share with the children to help them understand the processes of inventing: the breadboard (drawings), the model (not to scale and not necessarily working), and the prototype (the first working item). All children did not necessarily follow this format and did not always end up with three components. Most children made a prototype first and then did the drawings. It seemed most often that it was easier for them to make something. Children who created especially fanciful inventions such as an automatic baby changer and fiber armor had only drawings, with no model or prototype.

We were fortunate enough to have two inventors visit and share their descriptions of their own inventing processes. Brian Duerer's invention was a simple frame saver for a bicycle, which would save the frame of a bike from being scratched while being transported on ferries. Brian Costello's invention was a sophisticated and speedy aqua-car. The contrast in technology used by the two inventions was important to show the children. Useful inventions could be complex or simple. But the process that both inventors went through was similar. They talked about their successes, but they also talked about their failures. This helped the children understand that frustrations and mental blocks are common to adults as well as to kids. The children loved talking with the inventors and seeing the breadboards, models, and prototypes. The children were able to see the actual frame saver, and they saw a video of a test run of the aqua-car. The two Brians gave our children the encouragement they needed to forge ahead in their own inventing processes.

Partway through the invention project, we had a critique. The children brought to their small groups what they had accomplished to that point. This meeting gave them an opportunity to see what others had done, share their projects, and get each other's advice on how to make their inventions better and where to go next. This time also gave us an opportunity to see how the projects were coming along. In individual conferences, we were able to help the few children who were floundering. For a few children, the concept of inventing something was difficult. Just talking to us about different ideas was enough to get them started, and a few needed our help to develop a possibility identified in the conferences.

During their personal invention process, the children were required to keep journals. We wanted them to keep a written record of their ideas, drawings, and activities. This midpoint critique showed the shortcomings of their recordings. The assignment appeared to be too vague for many kids to understand. They needed us to identify specific questions they could address in their daily entries. Using this information, we identified some questions they could use as guidelines.

The culminating activity of the unit provided each student with an opportunity to make an oral presentation to the entire class plus a few visitors. Children signed up for 3- to 5-minute time slots on one of the three final days. Working again in our small groups, we identified information that students needed to include in their presentations as well as some examples of ways they might make their presentations. We provided students with practice time, and some of them became impressive salespeople in their pitches to sell their inventions. In a few cases, the kids seemed ready to buy items on the spot.

From the outset, the upper unit team emphasized students sharing their work in both informal discussions and in more formal presentations in front of a group. We believe that sharing ideas in public presentations provides experience with skills that are important for our students to develop. For some children, public speaking is an easier way to express themselves than writing. We urged them to write in their journals about these first public speaking experiences. For some it came easily, and for others it was more difficult. "I got nervous during the oral report because everyone was staring," said Bob. Marcy replied, "It was embarrassing standing up in front of 42 kids in the class, plus the second graders." Ian had a different viewpoint, "I could have kept talking. I know they liked my invention."

We found very little evidence of parents taking over invention projects even though most of the kids' work was done at home. We knew that parents were involved, but their contributions were more in terms of exchanging ideas than making the actual model. We noted that our younger children seemed to be more willing to take risks with ideas than the older students, who seemed more self-conscious about looking foolish in front of each other.

LEONARDO DA VINCI EXHIBIT

As indicated at the beginning, the seed of this unit was an exhibit of Leonardo da Vinci's inventions at the Musée de Beaux Arts in Montreal—less than 2 hours away. We had made a preview trip to make sure the show was appropriate for our children. Happily, the exhibit offered a wonderful opportunity for kids to see his writings, drawings, and numerous models of his inventions.

Before going on this field trip, we read aloud from a biography of Leonardo. We also showed pictures of his inventions, and the kids guessed how the inventions might be used. This speculation led to informative discussions about the inventions. We were all amazed at the number of inventions he had created and how advanced his ideas were for his time.

We decided to take the guided tour that the museum offered for children. This tour turned out to be geared more to adults than to children, and many of our kids became bored. The children behaved themselves anyway. They tried to be attentive and asked questions. Unfortunately, the tour guide's first language was French, so she had difficulty understanding our children's questions. We decided that next time we'd plan our own tour that would include some questions to discuss and a treasure hunt. When children are engaged in active looking, they take away more insights and understanding.

Despite the tour, however, children's comments were positive and reflected learning. Jerry reminded us, "That was the first scuba diving tank." Another was amazed that "Leonardo wrote everything backwards." Mark was impressed that "Leonardo de Vinci invented the first tank, but it was never built." We had covered these bits of information in class, but the field trip made them real and believable for students.

For some children, the museum trip was an incidental part of the trip to Montreal. Walking around the city, seeing the "tallest buildings I have ever seen," and visiting a city bigger and larger than nearby Burlington (population under 40,000) were "really something." Shopping for souvenirs and cruising the streets added memorably to this adventure.

RESEARCH REPORT

We wanted the unit to include reading and formal writing, so we assigned a research paper about one inventor or invention. This work gave children an opportunity to pick a topic of personal interest. Using their topics, we could teach them the mechanics of writing a research report. An advantage of having multiage groupings was that more advanced students could assist children who needed help in locating and organizing information. We were able to work most closely with students who were our least experienced and confident writers. The grouping also allowed the free exchange of ideas and suggestions. Our survey at the end of the unit showed that although this assignment wasn't particularly popular, the children felt that it was important. They also reported that they had learned a lot from their reading.

SURVEY

As we had lots of different activities in this unit, we felt it was important to have a system for keeping tabs on how children thought the unit was going. Therefore, we would periodically survey them in group discussions or in writing. We wanted to know how the unit was going and what kids liked and didn't like. We would use this information to modify our direction of this unit as well as that of future integrated studies. At the end of the unit, we gave the children a final survey that asked them to rate on a numerical scale all the activities, how well they liked the activities, and which experiences taught them the most. The last part of the survey asked direct questions. Two of the questions were the most revealing, even though they were the hardest for the children to answer: "How do you learn?" and "What did you learn about yourself in this unit?"

I could do a lot that I didn't think I could do.
I learned that you don't always get it on the first try.
I learned that my brain can do a lot after all. That shows that I am
    not dumb.

We concur.

Chapter  14

Garbology

Jane Vossler and Terry Moore
Essex Middle School, Essex Town

On a warm fall day in Essex, Vermont, 12 sixth and seventh graders set off on a novel mission. They marched along a dirt road looking for garbage. "Oh, look," someone shouted, "a piece of cloth." Mark dashed into the underbrush, grabbed the rag, and threw it into the plastic bag already half full of trash.

Along the sides of the road, they found beer cans, plastic bags, scraps of paper, part of a car bumper, an empty antifreeze can . . . the lists went on and on. One group tallied 130 different items. Another group reported the greatest weight. In addition to their two bags of garbage, they had found an abandoned car and a refrigerator complete with a bottle of salad dressing! Nathan, who lived near that road, said, "We found stuff I never dreamed was down there. I knew there was trash there, but not that much!"

Thus, we began our study of Garbology. After the two of us had planned for several weeks, we were under way. Still, the planning was not completed, and that made us a little anxious. There's always a tension between advanced planning and flexibility, between carefully stated goals and objectives and flying by the seat of your pants. How do you balance structure and spontaneity? How do you get a project to flow and still achieve your goals? How could we be sufficiently in control and ensure that the unit was truly owned by the students? We were to wrestle with these fundamental questions throughout the project.

Why garbage? We were looking for an environmental issue, one that would easily combine science concepts with social issues. The previous spring, the Vermont state legislature had passed a controversial solid-waste bill that taxed private landfills, required landfills to install expensive liners by 1991, and encouraged regional planning and recycling. The newspapers were filled with articles about these issues. Local leaders debated whether to join a regional planning group. Nationally, the garbage barge out of New York City had become infamous. It seemed that with both local and national attention focused on the garbage issue, it was a hot topic to pursue. As a society, finding solutions to today's problems of what to do with what we have left over will not be easy. Chances are good that when these young adolescents are voters, people will still be debating the issues, and the solutions will eventually affect everyone. We wanted to heighten student awareness so that in 10 years they'd be the ones attending and speaking out at town meetings and public hearings.

In the summer, during the initial planning for this project, we had decided on four main questions that we wanted our students on the Odyssey team to address and, as far as possible, to answer:

What do we produce?
What do we do with what we produce?
Why is there a problem?
What should we do about the problem?

Although our plans for specific activities shifted as the project progressed, these four questions remained the structure into which we fitted everything we did. Even though there were a number of late afternoons when we sat down to plan for the next day, in general we knew where we were going because of these questions.

Two weeks before the project was due to begin, the two of us and Ed McGuire, our student intern, sat down to plan the first week. The Odyssey Team was composed of 35 students with whom we worked on the major academic subjects. We could schedule the garbage study project for 90 minutes each day. For 10 minutes, which seemed more like 10 hours, the three of us sat immobilized. Thoughts of abandoning the project whirled through our minds until Ed suddenly said, "Maybe we should start with the home study." That seemed so obvious once he said it! We started thinking along this track, and week 1 slowly began to take form. But we continued to be stuck on day 1. How should we start this project, which we wanted to be so exciting? The next morning, while standing in the shower, Jane thought of the idea of a garbage scavenger hunt. Terry had said something the day before about creating a game. And so it goes. We played off each other's ideas, and the result was a creative product that none of us working alone would have generated.

We began by challenging our students with, "How much trash do you think you can find on an Essex road?" The class of 35 was divided into three groups, one group for each adult. Each group chose a dirt road, and we were off. At the end of the allotted half hour, the groups had covered about three fourths of a mile and collected two huge bags of trash.

We hoped that this trip would stimulate kids to begin to think about the different kinds of trash that people discard. The next day, students categorized their roadside finds and then decided as a large group on the categories to use in their home study of Garbology.

The plan was for each student to collect data from home on the amount and kinds of trash thrown away in 1 week. We wanted students to deal with trash in a concrete, personal way and to see themselves as producers of garbage and thus previously unaware contributors to a larger social problem.

At one time, we had thought of simply giving students the categories for this study, but at the last minute we decided to take the time to let students generate their own. (This is a good example of how teachers' planning decisions evolve as a unit evolves). This approach was more interesting, but it was also more difficult. It was right before lunch, and 35 students were crowded into one classroom. They'd been sitting still for 45 minutes, and arguments flared as they struggled to reach consensus:

> Should we have a category for leaves?
> No, leaves aren't trash.
> Yes, they are.
> What about liquids? Are sour milk and leftover pickle juice considered foods or do they deserve a category of their own?
> Where does cat litter fit?
> How about tea bags?

Finally, we reached agreement. The seven categories we'd use were metal, paper, plastic/styrofoam, glass, liquids, food, and other (wood, rubber, cloth, and anything else we hadn't thought of). With a sigh of relief, we all headed to lunch. We teachers also noted that the kids' categories were more inclusive than those the three of us had thought up.

For the next week, everyone categorized and weighed their trash at home. Students wrote in their learning logs about how it was going.

Disgusting!
Much better than I thought!
The whole family is helping out!
Mom doesn't like having seven bags all over her kitchen.
My study is going well except my brother keeps dumping his oatmeal down the sink before I can weigh it.
Mom and Dad are really getting into this.

So there we were with piles of data: 35 families and the amount of garbage in each category for 7 days. Fortunately, our school has a computer lab, and students fed all the data into the computers. Using the *Appleworks* program plus writing their own program in *Basic,* they calculated how much garbage their families in Essex produce and then estimated figures for Vermont and the nation. When Jeff and Ryan computed the garbage production of the world, we discussed Third World nations and how it might not be accurate to project their garbage production from data gathered in our more affluent suburban community.

With our computer study completed, we had answered the question, "What do we produce?" Our search for the answer to the next question, "What do we do with what we produce?" took us first to the Essex landfill. Early in our planning, we had contacted Dennis Lutz, our town's public works director. Throughout the project, he was of immense help. We took the kids to meet him at the landfill on a damp and bleak October day. The kids had many questions as the bus pulled into the landfill: "Do you think it will smell?" "Will we see any animals?" "If we see something we like can we bring it home?"

Mr. Lutz greeted us with cider and doughnuts because he "wanted to dispel the image that most kids have of the landfill as an unpleasant place." Although many kids had been to the landfill before with their parents, none had had a personal tour. Back at school, students wrote their impressions. Mike, one of the class's most descriptive writers, wrote:

The huge yellow compactor roared over a mountain of garbage. Under its massive steel wheels were the sounds of bottles, boxes, couches, and toys being crushed to a pulp. Mr. Lutz started the tour of the wasteland by showing us where ash is supposed to be dumped. He revealed a mountain of it, dark and light, swirling up into the clouds in the soft wind. Then he took us down the road a little further and pointed out where at one time part of the road had been a huge, gaping hole, but had recently been filled in with trash and packed earth. We trudged along onto packed ground, with pieces of trash sticking out in many places. Just then, we were startled by the abrupt sound of beating wings, and a huge white wall of sea gulls flew up in a narrow escape from the compactor. . . .

Back in the classroom, we wanted to follow up on our trip by helping students to understand how toxic substances could leach out of landfills and contaminate water supplies. When water percolates through a landfill, soluble materials dissolve in the water and are carried into nearby surface water or groundwater. Although some of these substances may have been present in the waste to begin with, others are formed by the chemistry of decay. We felt this concept was essential for comprehending the entire solid-waste problem. Our plan was for each student to build a miniature landfill and simulate the process of leaching.

Terry demonstrated the procedure. A funnel blocked at the bottom with a loose wad of cheesecloth was used to represent the basin of the landfill. There were grins and giggles as students grated carrots and chopped tomatoes and alternated these with layers of sand in the funnel. It was hands-on, it was active, and although they complained ("This is gross!" and "Yuck! Smell Mike's tomatoes!"), they were curious about what would happen to their mini-landfills. Each day for a week, students poured small amounts of water through their landfills, collecting the leachate in beakers. Just before the smell became unbearable, an engineer from a local engineering firm came to test the runoff. Students were fascinated with the array of scientific equipment he used to test the water. They were startled that after only a week, the water was severely contaminated. "I'm really worried that we're polluting our drinking water," said Mark.

Kids were beginning to understand the operating procedures used at landfills today, but we wanted them to look at trash from a historical perspective as well. We couldn't seem to find any written material on this subject. This turned out to be fortunate because it forced us to come up with an alternative research plan: oral histories. Each student was told to interview three people: one aged 30 to 40, one aged 50 to 60, and one aged 70 or older. They were to ask three questions: When you were growing up, what did you do with your trash? How is your trash different now? What memories do you have of the dump you used? Before students began the assignment, we practiced interviewing techniques by role-playing, stressing ways to encourage interviewees to elaborate.

On the day the assignment was due, students were eager to share what they'd discovered. As they talked, we kept pushing them to recognize patterns in the diverse information they'd collected. Christian said, "The other day, I called my grandmother. She had some interesting stuff to say, like they fed most of their food scraps to animals and burned up stuff that was burnable. They never went to the dump. They just dumped the garbage they couldn't burn into a big pit in the backyard." Many students discovered the prevalence of backyard dumps, particularly in rural areas, but others found that garbage collecting has been in existence for longer than they had thought. Many of the oldest people recalled garbage collectors coming to their home. Thus, students learned to be wary of making premature generalizations. They also learned the importance of the age of the interviewees and where they had lived. Soon, when a student reported information, someone would quickly ask, "Well, was that in a rural or urban area?"

Brian didn't know anyone in the 70 or older age range, so he asked me if he could go to a local retirement home and interview some of the residents. We complimented him, "That's a great idea. Why don't you go ahead and organize it?" He made all the arrangements for a visit and talked three friends into going with him. Using the school's portable video camera, they taped eight residents who dressed in their Sunday best and recalled their trash memories. It's exciting to see kids take initiative, spin off from projects, and function so well outside the walls of the school.

Students interviewed a number of people who spoke about the sport of rat shooting. Carrie's grandmother recalled that she belonged to a gun club in high school. For practice before her meets, she'd often shoot rats at the dump. One student's grandfather told her that he used to take his dates to the dump. He'd use a .22 caliber rifle to shoot rats, sometimes getting up to a dozen in an evening. When he got married, his wife threw away the gun because she didn't want him going to the dump. Some people didn't shoot rats. They bet on them! Brett's grandfather told him that people used to gather at the city dump at night, when the dump man would set up a maze. Poor people would bring rats that they'd trained and put them in the maze. The rats would run to the end to get food, and people would bet on them.

As such stories were spun, students also began to get a picture of life in a less affluent time when people threw away less and packaging was less elaborate. Jason wrote:

I think the best story was my grandma's. She told me that nobody
threw away food or clothes. They always gave them to the people who
needed them. Everybody was poor. If you had leftovers, you would eat
them as soon as possible. Once her brother found a pair of skates at
the dump and gave them to her. She was so proud to have a pair of
skates.

Students realized that a home study 20 or 30 or 40 years ago would
have had quite different results than the one they had just conducted. We
were pleased with the history lessons learned but were even more pleased
with the communication that had occurred between generations.

From the past we jumped to the future. During our trip to the Essex
landfill, we'd learned that the present site would be operational for
approximately another 5 years. The issue of what to do with all the
trash that the students had weighed earlier would soon be pressing for
the citizens of Essex. As one of our goals was to produce informed and
involved citizens, a simulation of finding a new landfill site for Essex
seemed like a way to promote future involvement.

Committees were formed and given the task of recommending a
new landfill site. After a brief introduction to the concept of zoning,
students began brainstorming what they needed to know in order to
choose a site.

"How far does the landfill have to be from streams and rivers?" was
a common question. Their study of leachate from their mini-landfills
had convinced them of the importance of landfill location. Once they'd
compiled a list of questions, the public works director returned for
another visit to provide technical consultation and maps for students
to work with.

Following Dennis Lutz's presentations, students wrote in their
learning logs, as they did periodically throughout this project. Becky
commented, "I thought it was especially interesting when he talked
about the cost of making a landfill. And boy, is it expensive!" Carrie
learned that "There are a lot of steps in making a landfill and in finding a place for it." Ryan wrote, "I learned that it makes a difference if
the landfill is close to public water pipes or if there are wells."

Lutz also talked about the political considerations in finding a
landfill site. ("A perfect example of how real life is interdisciplinary,"
we thought. "The technical bumps up against the political.") He drew
a square on the board and surrounded it on two sides by houses. "Pretend this is an R2 zone," he said. "Maybe you and your family live
here." Many students indicated that they did live in an R2 zone. "Now
suppose I said this was the ideal site for a landfill. The soil is great. The
elevation is perfect. The accessibility . . . "

"Not in my backyard!" shouted one student in a spontaneous outburst. Lutz laughed and wrote "NIMBY" on the board. Several days prior to this, students had learned the acronym in a language arts lesson. Lutz acknowledged that the NIMBY factor is one of the most difficult to deal with in finding a site. Now that students had criteria to work with, they began evaluating sites. They remembered that Lutz had said, "There is no perfect site. You need to find an area that has more pluses than minuses."

Our two classrooms were filled with maps of all kinds—topographic, tax, soil, zoning, and public water line maps. "I never knew there were so many kinds of maps," said Amy. A visitor to our classroom during this part of the project would have seen students gathered in small groups on the floor, crouched over large maps of Essex. One student colored in rivers and streams. Another studied a soil map and shaded in all areas where the soil was type 1 through type 9. A third jumped up and hurried over to consult a zoning map hung on the wall.

"Measure how far it is to the nearest river," someone ordered, and his friend ran to get a ruler. "We can't put it there. That's an agricultural-residential zone." "Okay, well, how about there?"

Kevin described his group's work:

> My group has some pretty nice people in it. I enjoy working with them because they are cooperative and speak their mind if they have a problem. We have chosen two sites, but we're leaning in favor of the first one, which is in an I-1 zone. We like this spot because it has the best soil blend, a convenient location, and ideal elevation. The problems are that it's near a few people with wells. Also, people might not like it on the side of the road like we've planned.

Not all groups functioned as smoothly as Kevin's. There were arguments, compromises, and in one group, a minority report—just like in the adult world.

Mr. Lutz returned for a final visit when the groups were ready to present their final site recommendations. It was interesting that there were nine groups and seven different sites. As the presentations were made, students in other groups challenged the presenters to defend their recommendations. Each group was secretly hoping that they would be able to recommend a site that Lutz hadn't thought of. He told them that several sites "had possibilities" (politically, that was the most he could say), and he pointed out technical problems with other sites that students had no way of knowing about when they did their simulation.

As we listened to the kids' persuasive presentations and assertive demands for facts, we could picture these same students 10 years from now standing up at a town meeting to ask pointed questions and propose solutions to difficult problems.

Students were also involved in other ways with the topic. We spent several days making anti-littering posters, which we then hung up in the hallways. Over the course of a month, Jane read aloud a juvenile novel, *Mrs. Fish, Ape, and Me, the Dump Queen,* by Norma Fox Mazer, a wonderful story of a girl who lives at the dump with her uncle. The theme is what it's like to be an outsider and to be different. The kids also read articles from the newspaper on local recycling projects and magazine articles on the invention of the tin can and on how computer paper and microwaves contribute to the garbage problem. They also wrote business letters to local industries asking what they did with their trash.

One of our biggest problems was sorting through the huge volume of information and ideas so as to choose which activities to pursue. It seemed that we had enough ideas to study Garbology for several years. As it was, we studied it for approximately 4 months—the longest integrated study we'd ever done. If we were to change anything about this unit, it would be to shorten it, even though choosing what to eliminate would be difficult.

To bring closure to the unit, we had to deal with the final and perhaps the most difficult question, "What should we do about the solid-waste problem?" First, we took two more field trips. We visited Gardner's Supply Center, which had recently initiated a composting project for the city of Burlington. Residents of the city and surrounding areas brought their leaves and grass clippings to the center, where they turned it into compost over the winter to sell to gardeners in the spring. It was exciting to see research in action and to talk with dedicated people who were on the cutting edge of change—especially as it related to preserving our community's environment.

From the compost piles we went to a warehouse at the other end of the city to see a salvage operation. Students were fascinated by the huge stacks of newspaper, the scrap metal, and the bundles of old clothes. "We have three markets for clothes," said the owner. "Some of it is sold to make paper, some to produce rags, and the best stuff is sold in Europe as secondhand clothing." Students left with firsthand information about recycling for profit and its major problem: finding suitable markets. On the final evaluation of Garbology, a majority of students cited these field trips as their favorite activities.

Next, we organized students into four- and five-member groups to pursue possible solutions to the solid-waste problem. Groups focused on topics such as fast food packaging, paper in school, composting at home and at school, styrofoam in school, incineration, liners for the landfill, and compaction.

On one particularly memorable day, Dean rushed up, his face glowing with excitement and urgency. "I've got to go call the big guy at McDonald's," he explained. "I think some of these figures on daily sales are wrong. We've got to make sure this information is accurate, you know." Receiving a nod of okay, he tossed the words back over his shoulder as he dashed down the hall to the phone. His group was investigating the use of styrofoam, and calling the regional manager of McDonald's was one phase of their research. Meanwhile, other students stood in line to use the phone. Keith was calling the public works director to inquire about landfill liners. Meredith was calling a local garbage collector to set up an interview about compaction. It seemed as if everyone was going in a different direction. We let them go.

In addition to using human resources to find information, the whole team visited the Fletcher Free Library in Burlington, the largest public library in our area, to exercise their research skills in an unfamiliar setting. They combed the card catalog, vertical files, *Readers Guide*, encyclopedias, and newspaper files. In an information-rich society in which the rate of increase of new knowledge constantly accelerates, we believe it is vital for our students to learn and continually practice skills of investigation so they can become independent, life-long learners.

Back at school, we pieced the research together. The group that was investigating the feasibility of recycling paper at school met in a corner of the room. Earlier, they had divided up the work; now they were back together to share what they'd discovered. Brett had tracked down the school custodian. "He said we throw away about 25 pounds of paper each day," Brett reported.

Tashianna had called the governor's office: "They told me the name of a recycling plant in Hardwick, so I called them, and they said they paid $50 for a ton of paper."

"How long would it take us to collect a ton of paper?" Casey asked. They made some calculations. "Sixteen weeks."

"How would we get all that paper to Hardwick?" Mark asked. "It's an hour's drive from here." "The custodians aren't going to have time to drive it there," said Brett. "We'll have to store it someplace."

"All that paper?"

Mark went over to talk to Ed, our intern teacher. Soon he was back. "He helped me figure out how big a building we'd need to store the paper. I'm going to design it now." He took out a piece of paper and began sketching. The others continued the discussion.

"Maybe there's a place closer than Hardwick."

"Yeah, maybe there's one in Burlington. But we've already checked the phone book. How can we find out?"

Setting reasonable expectations and then giving students the freedom to pursue knowledge down unknown paths are empowering to young adolescents. Letting them deal with people as well as print, allowing them to experience the struggles of learning how to work cooperatively, discovering things ourselves along with them—all of these trusts sometimes feel pretty risky. How much safer it appears to keep them in straight rows, memorizing facts for tomorrow's test. But how much more exciting, fulfilling, and authentic it is to travel down those unknown paths with them, exploring, discovering, and learning.

A December snow had fallen by the time we finally held our Garbology open house for parents to see our work. Students showed their parents how they did the computer study, led them through displays of the landfill site reports and learning logs, explained the maps, and watched themselves working in small groups on videotape. Then students presented their final reports. "I think it's great to see kids stand up in front of a group of strangers and make a presentation like this," commented Jeff's dad. "I wish I'd learned to do that when I was in school."

What did the students themselves make of Garbology? Casey wrote in her journal, perhaps summing it up for many:

> In the beginning I thought Mr. Moore and Ms. Vossler were turning us into garbage pickers. But I am realizing that garbage will become an even more important issue in the future because we're messing up this earth faster than we think. I want to learn a lot about the issue so I can help when I'm needed.

Several weeks after we had officially finished Garbology and had moved on to the next integrated study, which we titled International Traveler, Brian brought in an article from the local paper. "What do you think of this Vicon ash dump?" he asked, referring to a controversial local incineration project. Garbology was over, but the curiosity, the questions, and the searches for solutions continue.

Chapter 15

Carved in Stone

Patricia Stevens, Katherine Wilder, and Peter Reininger
Morristown Elementary School, Morrisville

"What are you guys doing?" We heard this question often as members of our class turned an empty classroom into a cemetery with their artistic handcrafted trees, gravestones, and a bridge. People asked us, "Why do you have a cemetery in the middle of the school?"

Middle grade students—in fact, most people—have an intense interest in death, but our class had experienced closer encounters with it than most kids their age. One of their classmates and his brother had been killed 2 years earlier in a car crash, and recently a popular high school student had committed suicide. These incidents had caused a good bit of anxiety, curiosity, and confusion. Talking about death in our small town was no longer taboo. Children reminisced about the deaths of relatives, friends, friends of friends, and pets. One boy told us he had seen a dead cat in the road: "I was scared. It made me think about my own death."

As their teachers, we listened and tried to be helpful, expressing empathy for their questions, showing our respect for their concerns. There was no doubt in our minds as to their interest in learning more about the topic. Their personal reflections, the philosophical nature of their observations in conversation, and their interest in their own existence and mortality evidenced a disposition for studying the topic.

We three also talked among ourselves, exchanging observations about how our culture handles this most inevitable of all human experience. We acknowledged to each other our own personal needs to explore this controversial issue, to understand it more fully, and to resolve some of its intimidating and morbid effects. We further realized that our community could provide many of the resources we needed to make a formal study of death: adults who had intimate experience in their families; local professionals such as clergy, lawyers, morticians, physicians, and a stonecutter/monument salesman; and cemeteries within walking distance of the school.

Given our society's general sensitivity about the topic, we had to first become much clearer in our own minds about what we wanted to accomplish in such a study. What were appropriate educational goals for such a unit? We visited a cemetery, looked around, and asked, What can our students learn here? We noted the art, cultural symbols, abbreviations, epitaphs, ethnic names, life spans, and economic and historical differences represented by the type and treatment of memorials. We spent a provocative afternoon in the cemetery and wished we could have stayed longer. We left with rubbings we made to be used as examples for our students at a later date. We also left with great enthusiasm for this unit and confidence that we could teach it well.

Of course, we also confronted the challenge of justifying the unit in terms of our school's established curriculum, which didn't include death as a topic. An examination of the scope and sequence satisfied us, however, that this particular topic touched on skill objectives included in every middle level discipline—confirming it as a natural topic for an integrated study. Having worked out to our own satisfaction and to the satisfaction of our principal that we had created an appropriate unit of study, we explained our intentions to our students and requested support from their parents. Then we got started.

On the first day of the unit, the three of us plus our student teacher greeted our 72 students in a darkened room with only a burning candle for illumination. Thus, our unit began with a scene from Mark Twain's *Tom Sawyer*. With an appropriate musical background, we presented the traditional mystifying, spooky feelings commonly associated with a cemetery. From the laughter at the end of the skit came the inevitable question, "Why did you do this?" Immediately, we initiated a brainstorming session, asking: "What do you know about death and dying, and what would you like to know?" As we had hoped, what students wanted to know paralleled the activities we had selected from our own earlier brainstorming session.

Some of the kids' most urgent questions were:

What happens if someone forgets to write a will and dies?
What about mausoleums?
What happens after a death?
What do people at the morgue do?
What happens when the graveyard is full?
Why does a person have to be buried in a graveyard?
Where do the cremated person's remains go?
Where are gravestones made?
Why is there a wait before the dead are buried?
What happens at a wake?
What are the buildings in a cemetery for?

With the students' contributions, we put together a time line for the unit, listing daily activities. Permission forms for cemetery field trips were sent to parents. We began to teach about the cemetery as a resource. We put up bulletin boards with epitaphs the students wrote and gravestones they designed. We talked about some of the causes of death, life spans, and differences in what people do at funerals according to religion and ethnic differences. Students commented:

I'm a little excited and a little bit scared.
I want to do this unit because I want to learn about it.
I don't know too much about the dead.

"How do you feel when you are in or near a cemetery?" we asked our class. We found the answers differed as to whether it was during the day or at night. Many of our students had used the cemetery for bike riding and other fun activities. Some of them spoke about feeling sad, leading to a discussion about people's feelings concerning cemeteries. That session resulted in kids designing an interview to use with their parents and others.

"I did the interview with my dad," reported one student, "and he came up with different answers than I thought he would." Most of our students were surprised at their parents' comments. The kids seemed to have expected that their parents would feel the same way they felt about cemeteries: that they were horrible, macabre, and scary. They seemed reassured by their parents' responses. They also learned that their parents were interested in what we were learning, such as the history in the cemetery. Some of them shared their kids' sad feelings when visiting the cemetery and seeing graves of members of their family and other people they had known. Some of them spoke about feeling a sense of peace at the cemetery. We realized that this unit was providing a good opportunity for parents and kids to talk with each other about a vital value that parents and children ought to discuss. Our kids were also talking a lot with each other about it.

Our first outside resource person was a stonecutter, salesman, and owner of a monument business. He brought the blueprint design for the stone that marks the grave of our deceased classmate and his brother. The blueprint created immediate interest in his presentation. We all learned many things from this man.

Dying is not cheap.
I never knew the cemetery was the second best place to get information about a person. (The town clerk's office was given as the first.)
I learned that granite comes in colors.

This final comment was in response to the many different samples of granite that our guest displayed for us, including black African granite. Everyone wanted to know if Vermont granite is the best. We also learned that for years, Vermont was the granite center of the world.

On our first trip to the cemetery, students collected data from the gravestones: epitaphs, ages of the deceased, types of stone, shapes of stones, cemetery patterns, ethnic names, cultural symbols, military information, and secret order insignias. Back at school, we organized this information for use in different subject areas. "I can figure out this man's age from when he was born!" was heard in math class.

Following that first cemetery trip, we presented our students with three project choices: design a cemetery and build a model of it in an empty classroom; write and present a dramatic skit; or collect anecdotes to present with a tour of the cemetery, emphasizing its resources. Time was scheduled each day for working on these group projects.

"I would have to be at least eighteen to write a legal will," one student wrote in her journal after listening to a lawyer who came to our class. "I think it is kind of dumb because if I die before I am eighteen I want to be able to give my money and my possessions to the people I want to," wrote another. "Yuck! I wouldn't want that job," grimaced a student during the mortician/funeral director's talk. These were other responses:

I learned that during cremation the flames never touch the body.
I think he must be strong to work with bodies. I would never touch a dead body.

You can donate your body to science.
It's cheaper to die than go to college.
I wish when I die that I could just be put in the ground with no
     coffin, so I could become part of the land.
I was surprised a mortician had to go to college.
It is cool to learn what can be done to a body.

Journal entries following a discussion of responses to death included:

Today the guidance counselor told us about grieving. It really made me realize what it would be like to have my mom die or someone who is very close to me die.

I learned that it is okay to have anger, guilt, and sadness and to tell someone. I had these feelings when my grandpa died last year.

I learned how to cope with death today.

People respond differently to death.

We made a second trip to the cemetery to do gravestone rubbings. Under a blue October sky with a wind just strong enough to make doing rubbings a challenge, our students used crayons and shelf paper to make relief impressions of epitaphs and symbols. "I found my grandfather's grave," called out one student. "Here's someone with a name just like mine," sang out another. When we returned to school, we decorated our rooms and the hallway with these artifacts.

The students fine-tuned their final projects and then made presentations. The whole school enjoyed our "classroom cemetery," although one boy complained, "He shouldn't have put me on a gravestone without my permission." The play they wrote about ways to deal with death was a great success. "I liked the play. I was in it," wrote one student on her evaluation of the unit. "Being only the announcer was not too much fun, but the play was wonderful," wrote another student.

Other comments taken from the final evaluation reflected a positive experience:

I enjoyed doing this unit because I am not afraid of death any-
     more.
I learned to take every day, day by day and not think every day,
     "When am I going to die?"

The rubbings were fun.
Not all people live a full life is what I learned.

Everyone agreed that collecting information from the cemetery itself made the unit an especially valuable experience.

Results from the inquiry we made about our parents' attitudes toward the study were extremely positive, with only one negative response (expressing concern over the "morbid nature" of the topic) out of 45 returns:

Interesting way to tie many concepts together.
It's a reality of life.
I felt good that the children were introduced to this subject.
Sixth graders need to deal with this.

As we finish writing about this teaching experience, we are already planning our next integrated study. We find it such an effective way for students at this age to learn that we hope to teach several more during the school year. For Exploring, a unit we are planning for next fall, we will have an overnight camp-out in the woods behind our school. But that's another story.

Daring to Dance . . . or Not

Chris Stevenson and Judy F. Carr

As observant, experienced teachers, we know what young adolescents engaged in real learning do: They talk to each other about their work, swapping ideas, making comparisons, exchanging questions. Kids take initiative, demonstrate self-direction, and show responsibility. They also show each other how to do things, how to approach a problem, and how to get more help when it is needed. When they reflect on each other's ideas as well as on their own, withhold final judgment until all of the data are in, and show their capacity for dealing with ambiguity, we know there is certain learner involvement.

The teachers participating in this project understand and respect the enormous potential of their young adolescent students. Whether working alone or together, these teachers have striven to create a context in which their students could more fully realize their inherent worthiness as learners, thinkers, workers, and citizens while they also have adventure and fun in ways that are appropriate to this transitional time of life.

Nevertheless, successfully engaging and teaching these spirited youngsters remains much more ambiguous work than many realize. At its best, there is variety in the kinds of work they do. The image of children sitting placidly in rows quietly doing the same work is a false illusion of active learning. Kids continually change, sometimes dramatically and sometimes so subtly that their new developments may go unrecognized. They may be exhibiting new intensities about each other. Many of them seem to struggle constantly with impulses that, when acted on, get them in trouble either at home or at school or both. Possibilities for turmoil are always present whenever they're together. Home life for many is in shambles. Large numbers of kids know first-hand the tensions associated with parents living apart or both working such long hours that family life is reduced to a minimum or dissolves altogether.

Even in the best of schools, the intensity of this all challenges the most able, committed, best-prepared teachers. Making these several school years momentous in ways that can lead kids to continue developing their minds, bodies, and souls in directions that are compatible with the educational values that our schools are charged with accomplishing is a formidable but critical mission. But it is also a possible one. Whether this mission is accomplished in any particular classroom or school, however, depends more on the teacher's vision and commitments than on any other factors.

It is probably true that no career is immune from tension. Teaching, however, exposes us to endless possibilities for having to deal with serious issues in other people's lives. How some teachers keep going, giving their best to kids, often under very difficult circumstances, is inspiring. Clearly, some of them are energized by young adolescents and their grapples with growth. By being who they are, these teachers help the rest of us keep ourselves from becoming complacent, too sure of ourselves, too self-important. Luckily, many such teachers are at work in middle grade classrooms. A few have written about their experiences and insights.

Kim Marshall's wonderful, poignant account of teaching 11- and 12-year-olds at the M. L. King School in Roxbury, a mostly Black Boston ghetto, recounts a culture that is adversarial in the extreme to children's attitudes toward self-improvement through schooling (1973). His kids were confronted daily with discrimination and rejection. Their living context was intimidating at the least, and at its worst it was violent and chaotic. They suffered abuses of every imaginable kind. They were destined to lead lives without very much opportunity and few advantages beyond the toughness that each youngster had to acquire in order to simply survive from one day to the next. In spite of so many adversities, however, children arrived at his classroom every day ready to accept or toss back whatever he dished out:

> Yet, here they are, full of life, their hearts and minds belonging only to them, every one of them yearning, reaching out to be someone. Instead of weakness and defeat, I have found toughness and vitality . . . eager and full of potential, endearingly alive. . . .
> Marshall, 1973, p.183

It becomes evident from Marshall's account of his 3 years in that inner-city setting that children's resiliency to the misfortunes in their personal lives both enlightened and sustained him. Their toughness steeled his resolve to explore lots of ways to meet them on their terms and complement their eagerness to thrive.

Another exceptional middle grade teacher, Nancie Atwell, has also written explicitly and inspirationally about how much she learned from her students about how to best serve them (1987). Although her students in Boothbay, Maine, did not face the same hardships that Marshall's students knew, they nonetheless shared the transition issues that all young adolescents experience. Not only did her time with them confirm her recall of the intensity of her own adolescence, but it became an opportunity for her to learn how to help them manage day to day.

> Surviving adolescence is no small matter; neither is surviving adolescents. It's a hard age to be and teach. The worst things that ever happened to anybody happen every day. But some of the best things can happen, too, and they're more likely to happen when . . . teachers understand the nature of . . . kids and teach in ways that help students grow.
>
> Atwell, 1987, p. 25

What is especially noteworthy is that both of these perceptive, responsive teachers respected their students' time of life and the issues that made it so challenging for them to manage. Both teachers used their couple of years with their kids as opportunities to learn from them about how to make their middle years of schooling productive and relevant. In pursuing this opportunity, these teachers chose more difficult paths than we are accustomed to seeing teachers choose.

Middle grade teachers have not always written so positively and optimistically about their experiences, however. The challenges of teaching children who can be so capricious can overwhelm, and an occasional teacher-writer describes the experience pessimistically. Such a teacher-writer is James Herndon, who has invested more than 2 dozen years in working in a California junior high school. Herndon's gift for telling about his experiences works well to amuse and entertain, but the anecdotes and reflections he shares reveal his cynicism (1985). Sadly, he has apparently not found ways to achieve the kind of credibility that makes it possible to consistently break through the barriers that appear to distinguish schooling from authentic learning.

Herndon's account of teachers' lounge dialogue on the last day of a school year reflects an all too familiar frustration, succumbing to fatalism:

We are reminded that these same subjects come up on this last day every year. They are exactly the same. Nothing has ever been done about them. Nothing will, or can, be done about almost everything that really drives us crazy in our lives as teachers. No matter how we perceive the school, no matter what we think about how the education of junior high students should go, no matter what we think about how to deal with the students who don't make it in our school, or the kids that do make it—and our opinions on these subjects are anything but unanimous—we know that nothing real will ever be done to change or even ameliorate these conditions. They are permanent.

                                                                    Herndon, 1985, pp. 24–25

Thankfully, Marshall and Atwell not only found ways to change the conditions that they and their students found themselves in, but they also documented their processes and published accounts that have inspired others of us to do the same. The descriptions of integrated curriculum projects in this book have grown out of our attempt to create and document some learning opportunities not often found enough in middle level schools. Much of our courage for making the difficult choices that innovative efforts force is derived from the inspirational writings of Marshall and Atwell, plus the examples of many teachers we've encountered in our own work who are very much like them but who had not until now written about their work.

MATTERS OF CHOICE

Popular beliefs notwithstanding, teachers have a good bit of choice about what they teach. The largest single study of contemporary American education showed that although curriculum guides and instructional programs are usually provided, teachers continue to exercise a great deal of authority and discretion over not only what to teach but also over how it will be taught (Goodlad, 1984). Our informal inquiries with Vermont teachers confirmed that they were generally free to select and to organize curricular topics according to what they believed would best serve their particular students.

The teachers in this project presented themselves as curious to explore some new ways of teaching, eager to swap experiences, and willing to commit themselves to a regimen for carrying out and describing their work. Their responses throughout the project exuded their willingness to try out some ways of teaching that differed from the usual. To a person, they also exhibited a readiness to create experiences for their students that went well beyond just mastery of subject matter. At the outset, we drew inspiration from written accounts of other teachers' exploits.

For example, Jan Phillips' account of 11- and 12-year-olds studying a wide variety of issues relating to the planned construction of a dam on the Meramec River in Missouri stands as testimony to a teacher's decision to try out and go beyond what others believed was possible (1978). Through firsthand exploration and inquiry, those students were able to grasp many of the environmental and local political issues germane to the dam. They learned by reading, interviewing citizens affected by the proposed dam, comparing positions reported in newspapers, and drawing together data from all sources to develop personal positions. They also learned how to spelunk and how to use topographical maps.

Perhaps no contemporary teacher has written more clearly and reassuringly about issues relating to trying out than Eliot Wigginton (1985). His inspirational account of the often difficult choices he has confronted over the last 20 years reassured us that adolescents' potential for scholarship requires that their experiences go beyond classroom walls, textbooks, and conventional testing. The many fascinating volumes of *Foxfire* stand as tangible evidence of the high quality of academic work and personal growth that result when learning is authentic. Reading Wigginton's account also leaves certain notice that for kids, both good scholarship and personal fulfillment are extremely dependent on teachers' choices, decisions, and actions. From the very beginning, Wigginton confronted the evidence of meaninglessness in the prescribed curriculum in his school. He responded to circumstances by studying his students for evidence of their development and interests, weighing the risks and opting to try out an innovative, alternative plan based on how his students perceived their world. He never dreamed how far such responsiveness and ingenuity would take him and his students, nor did he suspect that he would so profoundly influence so many other teachers.

It is the courage of such teachers as Marshall, Atwell, Phillips, and Wigginton to "push the envelope" of accepted practice that inspired us. Sharing what they learned from trying out innovations encourages the hope that through similar innovations we can learn how to serve kids better in the middle grades. The variable conditions of middle grade teaching and young adolescent learning are simply too vast to be reducible to prescriptive routines for anything more than selected expositions, which by their nature require direct instruction.

In this project, we had one important benefit that the preceding innovators lacked: We had each other's support. We came together one evening to share some ideas and then returned to our separate schools to contemplate the possibilities. The atmosphere in some of our schools supported innovation and risk taking; that of other schools thwarted them. Even in schools in which we found encouragement, we still confronted no shortage of the challenging factors already described. Although some of our original group opted not to join us in this collaboration, those whose work has been described in the preceding chapters chose to do so because they were convinced of the value and challenges of such studies for their students and for themselves. They saw themselves as tryouts.

From our exchanges as well as from focused inquiry conducted by our colleague Ken Bergstrom with more than 100 other middle grade teachers, factors emerged throughout this experience that we all agreed were germane to the success of our projects. These factors merit every teacher's thoughtful attention and response, but teachers who resolve to pursue integrated studies of the type described in this book should be especially attentive to these factors.

Factor 1: Ensuring Developmental Appropriateness

There's no question that integrated teaching provides opportunities for rich, personally relevant learning. Because choices about which topics to study and how topics might be developed rely to a large extent on students' interests and choices, subsequent learning opportunities tend to be more inherently interesting than topics arbitrarily imposed without choices.

Achieving functional matches between instruction and developmental readiness is a tricky proposition, however. Therefore, the teacher must rely heavily on students' candid accounts of what they understand and can do, as well as what is beyond them. Individual needs and learning styles can be accommodated only through student-maintained records and documentation. Emphasis is on students becoming involved on their own terms and at a level at which they believe they're progressing. Monitoring a study in terms of its propriety for young adolescent students' development is, therefore, an essential component of integrated studies.

Factor 2: Promoting Collaboration

Working closely and creatively with colleagues on such worthwhile adventures as these studies is rewarding in lots of ways. We drew strength from each other's ideas, and we got to know and rely on each other better through our shared commitment. But it has been the spirit of personal and professional responsibility that has been most fulfilling. We acted together in faith that we could transcend conventional practice in legitimate, worthwhile ways for our students. The confidence we've gained that we can continue to grow as teachers fuels confidence in ourselves beyond school, too.

Teachers are always searching for ways to get kids to work with each other in a healthy, cooperative learning environment that will promote social skills and class morale. Many teachers want to collaborate with colleagues as well as with their students. It is through these shared efforts that adults and children find new ways of knowing each other. Our experience has shown us that we must be the initiators if such collaboration is to occur. We must become the models that others will acknowledge and join.

Factor 3: Reflecting the World of Actualities

Educators and other citizens earnestly debate whether schools should present kids with an edited, sanitized version of our nation or whether we should portray it as it really exists. Because our integrated studies are firsthand investigations and reflections of real experience, students recognize the authenticity of their activity and become more interested in their work. They take informed positions on issues pertaining to their interests, and they express confidence in the processes of real learning.

This straightforward approach to education credits kids with real responsibility. It involves and engages them positively. They understand the need to learn and correctly apply discrete skills. They recognize why it is important to be accurate and thorough. They appreciate the actuality of real consequences for their actions and decisions. They experience in very personal ways the satisfaction of contributing something worthwhile to their community.

Factor 4: Presenting Knowledge Holistically

The tradition of departmental organization in middle level schools has created false divisions and barriers in the body of knowledge considered appropriate and accessible for middle level students. Kids have come to approach their studies as social studies or math or language arts rather than as topics that integrate the subject matter of several disciplines. For example, a unit about the Westward Movement, which in a traditional setting would likely be taught as just a social studies unit, might instead include mathematical ratios (between people and available land) and time-distance-speed calculations (in planning travel), homesteading technologies, personal health and nutritional issues for pioneers, classic literature related to expansion, and so on.

Making (or reestablishing) connections among the artificial categorizations of subject matter makes sense to us. This "whole topic" approach is what we have referred to as integrated studies. We believe that we and our students have covered more subject matter in greater depth through our integrated pursuit of topics. We maintained an ongoing vigil to call attention to the interconnectedness of all things. Traditional gaps between subjects ceased being an issue. It was always the topic itself that directed our efforts and created the flow that ensured our students had meaningful continuity through a variety of activities.

Factor 5: Having Fun

"It was fun!" On the surface, that comment about a formal learning experience might appear to trivialize the work. But to those of us who have come to understand the somewhat idiomatic language of our kids, such expressions have considerably deeper meaning. Kids let us know when the work has meant something to them, has expanded their learning, and has brought some satisfaction. When a young adolescent offers "fun" in an appraisal about schoolwork, the prudent inquirer knows that at the very least the respondent approves in some important ways, whatever the work may be that he or she has done. "Fun" usually means "success."

Therefore, an appropriate component in the rationale for an integrated study is to have fun in this sense. The units reported in this book were fun in that students spoke positively about many aspects of their experiences. It is human to enjoy activities and celebrate learning when the growth feels good, when learning is shared as adventure. For some of these kids, a new enthusiasm for learning was generated; for others, something more akin to regeneration was apparent. In all cases, the work accomplished was creditable, and the kids exuded enthusiasm and pride in their accomplishments.

Factor 6: Collaborating With Parents

Integrated studies provide new opportunities for teachers to create ways in which parents can work with their children. Much of the guidance that kids need are common-sense things that many parents already know, such as how to organize an activity, plan time, and locate resources. Furthermore, all students benefit from personal adult encouragement and support for their individual work and for the accomplishment of group projects. Because most of the unit is not predicated on the assumption that every student is doing and learning precisely the same thing at the same time, parents can support both their own children and other youngsters without apprehension that "I'm not doing it like the teacher."

An integrated unit always entails many details that parents can take responsibility for arranging. Parents are usually skilled in ways that can expedite a variety of aspects of a study, such as helping with field trips, getting help from other adults, setting up contacts with local resources, and keyboarding on word processors or typewriters. Parent involvement with their primary-aged children is common, but by the middle grades, parents tend to have fewer opportunities and less inclination to become involved. For some tasks, parents may work with their own children. Other times, they work on tasks that relate to the total project. It is especially helpful when parents serve as resources for children other than their own. These interested and able adults just might constitute teachers' most underutilized resource.

Factor 7: Involving the Community

Just as parents can become effective resources for teachers, integrated studies also offer a wonderful opportunity to garner more widespread community support. Every community is populated with people who have expertise in a host of areas. By involving them directly with the school in a special project, we expand our teaching resources as well as build valuable new relationships. Our integrated studies have shown that community people brought into the studies have come to better understand our students and the exigencies of teaching them. Those collaborations and exchanges have then expanded into more widespread favorable relations between community members and ourselves.

Factor 8: Gaining Collegial and Administrative Support

Sometimes the school context already provides collegial and administrative support. In most cases, however, the organizational structure and pace of schools militate against our use of each other's expertise and against potential encouragement for innovative instruction. Sometimes it seems that limited resources pit us against each other for teaching time, preferred classrooms or students, and resources.

Breaking out of customary teaching routines brings new legitimacy to an innovative teacher's plea for help from colleagues, however. It somehow seems easier to ask for help about a topic when it is not usually associated with the established curriculum. For example, someone who is more accustomed to teaching language arts but who wishes to tackle a unit on bicycles may be able to use help from colleagues who understand and can explain how a derailleur works or where to locate music that relates to bicycling. Several of our teachers reported that colleagues "who almost never speak to me" have asked about the unit and have occasionally even offered their help. Perhaps an intent to cultivate this kind of camaraderie and encouragement is reason enough to pursue teaching integrated units. As one teacher observed, "It shakes things up and keeps us moving."

Factor 9: Motivating and Stretching Oneself

Growth is the commerce of schools. The decision to develop something uniquely challenging for students—learning experiences that transcend the usual—provides an opportunity for teachers' growth as well. Self-improvement is essential for adults, too, not just for kids. Our experience teaches that when we resolve to accept challenges, we are personally and professionally rewarded. We have learned things not previously known to us, and that knowledge has proved to be intellectually satisfying as well as personally fulfilling. We have learned a lot about our children, about how they think and learn and work. We've also learned about how to better plan and orchestrate future integrated studies. But we've learned some valuable things about ourselves, too.

There is some truth in the expression that "Mr. X claims to have taught 30 years, but he's actually just taught 1 year 30 times." Certainly every one of us has favorite teaching topics and strategies, but we've learned the benefits of attempting completely new units. An important dimension of the work reported in this book has been our periodic gatherings to share our work. As one teacher put it, "I feel like I'm an artist who studies the masters but then returns to my studio to express what is uniquely me."

It feels terrific to take on something new and see our kids taking charge as learners and doers. Their enthusiasm for our ideas is always pleasing, of course, but the respect we find ourselves developing for their ideas is truly wonderful. Taking the kinds of chances these teachers took may not look particularly formidable to the reader, but putting oneself on the line always demands courage and pays off by building character. In brief, we've learned a lot about how we create ourselves not just as teachers but also as human beings.

DRUTHERS NOT TO DANCE

Why would anyone choose not to do integrated studies? There are probably as many reasons as there are teachers for decisions to continue existing school practices. If change were easy and risk free, however, there would be a great deal more innovation. Nevertheless, liabilities accompany change. We've learned that many teachers who are attracted to ideas such as integrated studies but who ultimately back away offer similar reasons, which merit mention. We aren't in a position to judge whether explanations are authentic reasons or rationalized excuses for decisions not to teach in the innovative ways reported in this book. What we are quite certain of, however, is that the teachers whose work is described in the preceding chapters overcame factors that might cause others to pull back.

Factor 1: Fear

Fear underlies much of any person's hesitancy to explore different or untried ways of doing anything. Many teachers are afraid to let go of professional habits that have brought them comfort in the midst of an onslaught of changing students and changing school policies. The variety and intensity of kids' personal changes, the unending array of often volatile emotional issues they bring to school, pressures from high school teachers to see that incoming students have covered specific material—all these and more quickly become overwhelming. Teachers who give in to their fear are inclined to stick to their routines and preoccupation with order and control.

Yet they also reveal their doubts and curiosities in commentary about their work—sometimes expressing feelings of guilt for failing to become more innovative. They may even admit that their teaching is missing the mark too often and that they need to explore and to take some chances. But they have a hard time actually doing so on their own if they don't have the self-confidence necessary to be venturesome. Courage seems especially hard to come by when self-confidence lags. A trademark of this syndrome is a rationalization that "my kids are low ability level" or "have poor study habits" or "read 2 or 3 years below grade level." However, teachers who react in these ways continue to be conscious of other possibilities, and they really do want to evolve their teaching practice. Sometimes, they express an uneasy hope that a new principal will take responsibility for making changes.

Factor 2: Lack of Support

Teachers who engage their students in integrated studies must often cope with pressures that come from widely varying and often unsympathetic public expectations and inadequate resources in a profession that seems compelled to carry out schooling in the cheapest way possible. Concerns about stepping on toes and other related turf issues have also been noted frequently as sources of tension involving antagonistic colleagues or administrators. It is difficult to take the risks that innovation requires when one's aspirations for an original unit are continually met with "50 Reasons Why It Won't Work."

Teachers in this project and many others elsewhere have managed, however, to rise above an absence of support and, in some cases, even active opposition. In one instance, a contrary colleague of one of the teachers in this project spread false rumors among parents that the students working on one of the studies reported in this book were "just playing, fooling around, not learning anything." Those accusations were shortly refuted by those same students, who demonstrated the viability of this innovation by their products, by their conduct of credible work, and by their interactions with adults—especially their parents, but also other community members. To the teacher rationalizing that he or she cannot pursue an innovation because of lack of support, we advise that no matter how small and seemingly insignificant an innovation may be, begin somewhere. The ultimate source of reassurance lies in accomplishments whereby students demonstrate the effectiveness of their experience.

Factor 3: Insufficient Planning Time

Integrated studies cannot be done well extemporaneously. They require ample planning time—especially during the first few units one creates and especially when more than one teacher is involved. When two or more teachers collaborate, extra time is required in order to develop fully the collaboration. It is important, therefore, to think expansively but start small, perhaps with a 1-day or week-long unit. Replicating an integrated study that has been developed and successfully implemented by someone else is a valid way to enter into this work.

We have also learned that some of the best ideas come gradually when teachers have several weeks to digest an idea for a topic and exchange evolving ideas. An advantage of the design process for the studies reported in this book was that the teachers involved began to explore possibilities for a host of topics in the summer, a couple of months before they actually taught their units. Even after a basic design was settled, they still needed to meet to review and coordinate details. There is no single formula for scheduling this kind of planning time, however. Not all of the teachers whose chapters are included in this book were provided with joint planning time during the school day, yet they did find time to get together before or after school, during lunch, or by telephone in the evening. Teachers have to carve out time within the conditions of their given context.

Factor 4: Level of Difficulty

Teaching an integrated unit is harder than such traditional direct instructional practices as lecturing and administering work sheets. It requires identifying a topic or theme, researching its possibilities, locating available resources, learning new teaching techniques, providing better documentation of student growth, negotiating with the school community, and coordinating all of these elements. Acknowledgment that the teacher doesn't have to be directing every child all the time in every activity can be especially difficult to accomplish. Planning that requires this level of conceptual thinking and this investment of time and energy appears simply overwhelming to many teachers.

Factor 5: Lack of Resources

It is always interesting to observe how quickly teachers' discussions of possible innovations turn to a presumed lack of financial resources as an obstacle to teaching an integrated unit: "There's no more money for buses! The art teacher won't share supplies! We can't afford it!" In most schools, money for field trips or guest presenters and other so-called extras is limited, to be sure. Sometimes, one has to give up a trip or attendance at a particular event because there's simply no way to pay for it. Yet a combination of common sense, flexibility, and willpower can override a paucity of costly resources.

On the other hand, when kids and their parents believe in the project, essential resources usually follow. It makes sense to ask for help and to make do with what can be obtained. Besides, most integrated studies are not appreciably more costly than traditional teaching. None of the units described in this book entailed exceptional expenses.

Factor 6: Inflexible Scheduling

Daily school schedules are often needlessly tyrannical, and those that control time in the middle grades constitute an assortment of every imaginable grouping and organizational scheme. In addition to self-contained classes and a (junior) high school bell schedule, programs may also be defined by a department-based itinerary or by interdisciplinary teams of widely ranging composition or multiage groupings. In Vermont, for example, where there are basically two dominant high school organizational schemes (7–12 and 9–12) and two dominant elementary schemes (K–6 and K–8), there are 27 different school organizational configurations that include one or more of grades 5 through 8. There is, therefore, no single prevailing model for organizing time.

Scheduling problems, expressed in terms of availability of time as well as of space, thwart integrated teaching, which thrives on extended blocks of time in the same work space. A place to work for more than one 30- or 40-minute period is often not available. Other teachers are not always willing to release students for extended activities. Sadly, some teachers may withdraw from a possible unit without ever discussing with colleagues just how the schedule and classroom spaces might be reconfigured.

Factor 7: Curriculum Expectations

Teachers are often distracted from thinking optimistically about student-centered integrated teaching by a preoccupation with the curriculum—the textbooks, topics, skills, and so on that "must be covered." Predetermined, preestablished curricula are seen as a reason—or excuse—not to consider further innovations. If there are already a formal scope and sequence to follow, there will not be time to pursue something above and beyond them. Students' performance on standardized tests is narrowly and naively associated with a need to stick to the curriculum. Teachers and administrators who are more concerned about high scores than about the needs, best interests, and broad learning potential of their students are especially quick to deny the efficacy of curricular changes.

There is no evidence that students who participate in integrated studies score worse on standardized tests than their counterparts who do not have these innovative experiences. Additionally, our studies typically embrace a far greater number of objectives typically found in scope and sequence frameworks than can be addressed through more lockstep approaches. Furthermore, integrated studies address overarching goals too often ignored by traditional curriculum—goals described earlier in the first chapter of this book.

Factor 8: Degree of Risk

Teachers' decisions about when to deviate from a sanctioned program of study and when to capitalize on events or topics that they believe are more likely to inveigle kids' interest and commitment to work are not made lightly. Their choices about what to study, how to go about pursuing it, and when to do so always entail some degree of personal risk because choosing an alternative topic may be construed by others as choosing against their colleagues, their superiors, and the experts. Quite obviously, undertaking the kind of risk inherent in a departure from the approved course of study requires conviction and courage—a willingness to live somewhat dangerously in terms of one's reputation among peers.

The unremitting worry is: What if it doesn't work? There may be no humiliation greater for a teacher than falling flat on one's face after going against the experts. It is easy enough to blame the kids or their home situations or the textbooks or the curriculum designers or even previous teachers when we stick to an externally established plan of study that doesn't work out very well. But when teachers put themselves on the line to undertake an alternative topic, responsibility rests more squarely on those who made the choice to live dangerously. This risk alone may be enough to dissuade an apprehensive beginner from pursuing a personal inspiration. However, as those who have taken these risks can quickly attest, the benefits to both students and teachers of participating in successful integrated studies make these studies well worth taking the chance.

Factor 9: Need to Readdress Evaluation

Because integrated studies involve students in many more individual as well as small-group and whole-group activities and learning, traditional evaluation methods (for example, regular tests, pop quizzes, and exams given to a whole class) make little sense. At the same time, teachers' need to know even more about what each student is doing and learning is greater than ever. Giving up the weekly test and needing to keep up with students more individually are challenges that innovative teachers must address.

Obviously, integrated studies require some new ways of thinking about this issue. We approached evaluation and assessment as different entities (Stevenson, 1992). The former consists of some of the familiar forms of testing, enhanced by lots of documentation in student-maintained files, work samples, interviews, and presentations. In all evaluation activity, we gave recurring attention to evaluation in light of what was expected, i.e., the original goals as explained to the kids. Assessment, on the other hand, was aimed at helping the teacher understand how the study was progressing according to kids' testimony. Conversations, interviews, letters, and teacher observations served that purpose. The need to create and use documentation, assessment techniques, and different approaches to evaluate learning deters some teachers from pursuing integrated studies.

Factor 10: Classroom Control Issues

Integrated studies require kids to take more responsibility for their own learning and for their own conduct. Much less class time is spent in teacher-centered, work-sheet-oriented, and textbook-oriented instruction. Thus, for teachers who have difficulty sharing authority with their students, approaching an integrated study means confronting in new ways what has been traditionally referred to as control and discipline. Emphasis on student initiative and responsibility produces much greater frequency and diversity of those teachable moments that mean so much to both kids and adults. Because these units usually take on a life of their own, kids also take on responsibility for their own lives more willingly. They like having the trust and independence to be more responsible for themselves. Prudent teachers regularly restructure grouping patterns according to kids' needs to work in a variety of group roles and to the requirements of particular activities.

Factor 11: Ennui

Sometimes people know the tune and the steps, and they even feel the impulse to dance. Yet they stay put, perhaps tapping a foot but passing up opportunities without fully confronting and understanding their own inertia. Is there something about our profession that approves uncritical obedience to the way things are and have been? Or is there a natural acceptance that mindless conformity is a necessary rule? In his exceptional analysis of the American public, Charles Silberman described much of what occurs in classrooms as a consequence of professional "mindlessness" (1970). There is something about the context of schooling that resists sustained, fundamental change in the way things have always been that appears to absolve many teachers of the kind of self-examination that is necessary to move the professional practice of education ahead.

REBUFFING THE INVITATION

A final factor in the decision of some teachers against innovation such as ours is simply a difference in beliefs about how children should grow and learn as well as about the responsibilities of schools and teachers.

Many earnest teachers envision the educational process in terms of behavioral approaches to the teaching of specific, preconceived curriculum. That orientation is toward centralized teaching and learning processes whereby all students are expected to learn basically the same things. Emphasis is placed on careful organization of the material to be learned, modeling, rehearsal of responses, and high performance on criteria-based tests. Although our projects included carefully orchestrated direct instruction for specific needs, our integrated studies were oriented toward experiential learning in small groups and by individuals according to their particular interests and orientation.

Possibilities for innovation in schooling have also been foreclosed as far as individuals who see schools as "good enough" are concerned. Such teachers usually see their task in terms of keeping order, covering material in the classes assigned, and supporting an occasional extracurricular activity. Their commitment is to a somewhat vague notion of the school as an enduring institution that "was good enough for me, so it's good enough for them. After all, I turned out all right." Sometimes, they are thought of as retired on the job. Such people are likely to treat a colleague's excited sharing and aspirations for an original innovative project with indifference at the least and with scorn at the worst. Fortunately, we've encountered relatively few middle grade teachers who are so intractable. However, it is also extremely unlikely they would have chosen to be part of work such as ours in the first place.

MAKING INTEGRATED STUDIES HAPPEN

It is the premise of this book that the decision to innovate requires a strong belief in and commitment to developmentally appropriate curricula for young adolescents. Nevertheless, the reality is that commitment alone does not ensure that middle level teachers will make such efforts on behalf of their students. The absence of enough concrete examples of successful implementation of integrated studies in the middle grades has made it all too easy for too many teachers to rationalize why they should not make changes calculated to better serve kids' natural interests and developmental needs.

The teachers in this project, on the other hand, have discovered numerous motivations that make it worth their while to take a chance. These teachers are spontaneous and supportive, they search for meaning beyond the facts, they reflect on the process of teaching, they are learners themselves, they encourage cooperation, they involve students in planning their studies, they demonstrate self-respect, and they go beyond everyday routines and obstacles to meet the needs of all their students. They are the teachers who we seek for our own children, the ones who embody qualities appropriate to all who truly educate. They are also the ones you have met in this book.

The heart of this project is found in the teachers' accounts of their experiences in these units. The charge to each teacher or team of teachers was simply to "tell your story"—that is, recount the unit as documented in teachers' journals, children's comments and writings, and photographs. For most of us, this writing turned out to be more difficult than we anticipated. Reliving experiences such as these in one's mind's eye is simple—even automatic—whenever we get together to talk shop. But telling it in written words in a coherent sequence is another matter, regardless of how much we read and write in the course of our lives. Yet the authenticity of the work flows from the pens and word processors of these writers. This final portion of the book has been subjective and personally reflective.

In the months that have passed since we undertook these projects, we have had lots of opportunities to share our work in faculty meetings, in-service workshops, summer institutes, and conferences. Some additional teachers have joined us, trying out integrated units of their own design. Indeed, more teachers have joined us than we imagined back when we started. We have also tackled some new units ourselves, many of which have been inspired by each other. And thus, the lives of countless other young adolescents and middle level teachers have been touched by some of our earliest ideas.

It has never been easy. Most of us teach in less than ideal situations. But perhaps in that reality lies the most important message of this book: It can happen. We made it happen. And you can, too.

REFERENCES

Atwell, N. (1987). *In the Middle: Writing, Reading and Learning With Adolescents*. Portsmouth, NH: Heinemann.

Goodlad, J. I. (1984). *A Place Called School*. New York: McGraw-Hill.

Herndon, J. (1985). *Notes From a Schoolteacher*. New York: Simon & Schuster.

Marshall, K. (1973). *Law & Order in Grade 6–E*. Boston: Little, Brown.

Phillips, J. (1978). "A Cave, a Dam, a River." *Phi Delta Kappan*. June, pp. 703-704.

Silberman, C. (1970). *Crisis in the Classroom*. New York: Random House.

Stevenson, C. (1992). *Teaching Ten to Fourteen Year Olds*. White Plains, NY: Longman.

Wigginton, E. (1985). *Sometimes a Shining Moment*. New York: Doubleday.

About the Editors

CHRIS STEVENSON was a teacher and teaching principal for young adolescents for sixteen years prior to his present position as Associate Professor of Education at the University of Vermont. He is the author of *Teaching Ten to Fourteen Year Olds* (Longman, 1992), *Teachers as Inquirers* (NMSA, 1986), and coauthor of *The Middle School—and Beyond* (ASCD, 1992; with P. George, J. Thomason, and J. Beane).

JUDY F. CARR is Director of the Professional Development and Outreach Center at Trinity College of Vermont. A former middle grades teacher and K–12 curriculum director, she is also Project Director for the Vermont Middle Grades Initiative, sponsored by the Carnegie Corporation of New York and the Vermont Department of Education. She is coauthor of *Getting It Together: A Process Workbook for Curriculum Development, Implementation, and Assessment* (Allyn-Bacon, 1992; with D. Harris).

Index